P9-DUM-208

ONLY HUMAN

WHY WE ARE THE WAY WE ARE

This book is dedicated to
Adam, Eve, and all the kids.

This Brown Paper School book was edited and prepared
for publication at The Yolla Bolly Press, Covelo, California,
during the fall and winter of 1982. The series is under the supervision
of James and Carolyn Robertson. Editorial and production
staff: Dan Hibshman, Barbara Youngblood,
Diana Fairbanks, and Joyca Cunnan.

Copyright © 1983 by The Yolla Bolly Press

All rights reserved. No part of this book may be reproduced in any
form or by any electronic or mechanical means, including
information storage and retrieval systems, without permission in
writing from the publisher, except by a reviewer who may quote
brief passages in a review.

HC: 10 9 8 7 6 5 4 3

PB: 10 9 8 7 6 5 4 3

Library of Congress Cataloging in Publication Data

Bell, Neill.
Only human.

(A Brown paper school book)
Summary: Discusses differences and similarities in
human beings, how we got to be the way we are, and why
we do the things we do.
1. Human biology—Juvenile literature. 2. Human
behavior—Juvenile literature. [1. Human biology.
2. Human behavior. 3. Anthropology] I. Clifford, Sandy, ill.
II. Title.
QP37.B44 1983   599.9   83-9826
ISBN 0-316-08816-1
ISBN 0-316-08818-8 (pbk.)

BP hc
BB pb

First edition. Published simultaneously in Canada
by Little, Brown & Company (Canada) Limited.
Printed in the United States of America.

ONLY HUMAN
WHY WE ARE THE WAY WE ARE

NEILL BELL

ILLUSTRATIONS BY SANDY CLIFFORD

LITTLE, BROWN AND COMPANY
Boston   Toronto

CONTENTS

INTRODUCTION

Sometimes it's hard to believe the way animals look and the kinds of things they do.

Animals come in all shapes and sizes. How can gigantic, big-mouthed hippos have such tiny ears? And, speaking of ears, what about the size of the ones of an African elephant? You could hide behind one of those ears and still have room left for a friend. There are animals so small that dozens of them could fit on the period at the end of this sentence, so tiny that they can be seen only through a microscope. Some of them even live inside our bodies without our knowing it (except for a few of them that make us really sick!).

The things animals *do* are even more amazing than the way they look. Bats sleep upside down during the day and fly by night, using sounds instead of eyes to keep from bumping into things. Beavers use their big front teeth to cut down the trees they need to build log and mud dams. Bees by the thousands live and work together in giant colonies. Raccoons have a habit of always washing their food, even if it has just come from a creek.

As strange as all these things sound, there is one animal so unusual that it can do all these things. (Well, most of them, anyway.) It finds its way around in the dark using sound, builds dams the way a beaver does, lives in colonies made up of millions of members, and spends more time fussing over its food than raccoons do.

This animal lives in practically every corner of the world and can be found in any zoo. There have been more pictures taken of it and more books written about it than any other living creature.

What animal is it? To take a look at one without waiting for your next trip to the zoo, just walk over to the nearest mirror. That's right, the animal is *Homo sapiens,* a human being, a person, you.

If you are curious about just what kind of animal we humans are, how we got to be this way, and why we do the things we do, this book is for you. Because it is also *about* you.

(Don't *you* sleep upside down?)

CHAPTER ONE
MAN ALIVE

You may not be used to thinking of yourself as an animal. Kids do sometimes get messages from parents, who compare them with nonhumans. You'll hear, "You are behaving just like an animal," or "Stop eating like an animal," or "Your room looks just as if an animal lives in it."

The fact is that we humans are just as much animals as any worm, toad, or pig. Man* is one of more than a million different kinds of animals living in the world today. We are unusual creatures, but we share many things with our fellow animals.

---

*"Man" here means the same thing as "human," not just grownup members of the male sex.

We are born, get hungry, eat, grow up, have children, and finally die—like all the other animals on the planet we call Earth. So if we really want to know more about ourselves, we need to know more about those other critters out there who are our relatives.

Small-Game Hunter

Poor Noah must have had an awful time keeping track of all the animals on his ark. Remember that there are more than a million—that's 1,000,000! —different kinds of animals. The scientists who study animal life (they are called *zoologists*) have the same problem: how do you keep track of a million different anythings?

Zoologists do it by answering questions about the way each animal is put together. The answers tell them in which ways animals are alike, and in which ways they are different. Then the scientists can divide the animals into groups, in the same way you sort your family's laundry. You begin with one big pile and sort it into smaller and smaller piles.

You can do the same thing with animals yourself, by becoming a small-game hunter. Look around your house and neighborhood for all the animals you can find there (don't forget to look for really small ones—ants, minnows, and worms are animals too). List the names of the animals, and write down beside each name the number of each of the following questions that you can answer with a yes.

ANTS ARE ANIMALS TOO!

1. Does this animal move around on its own?

2. Does it have a bony skeleton inside its body?

3. Does it have warm blood?

4. Is there fur or hair covering its body?

If you have trouble answering some of these questions, that's not surprising. It isn't easy to tell just by looking whether or not an animal has warm blood or a bony skeleton inside its body. That's why zoologists take a very close look at the animals they study—including the insides—and ask a lot more questions than the four we have asked here.

Even with only these four questions, you can sort out some important facts about your small game. Each animal can be put into the circles according to the yes answers you gave for the numbered questions. Any of them that don't belong inside the first (biggest) circle probably aren't animals at all, since all animals move around by their own power at some time in their lives.

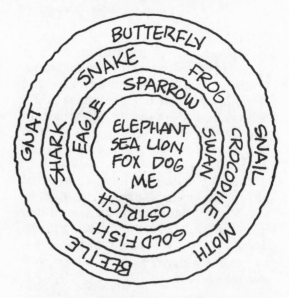

Not all of your animals will be included in the second circle. Because only those with backbones belong

10

there, that circle leaves out most of the animals of the world! Did you know that there are more different kinds of insects than there are all the other kinds of animals put together?

The third circle is smaller still because even fewer animals have warm blood. If you found a toad or a frog, for instance, it should not be included in the third circle because its body does not keep a constant warm temperature.

The last circle is the smallest. Very few of the world's animals have backbones, warm blood, and fur or hair covering their bodies. But you see many of them around you. One reason you do (apart from the fact that they are larger than most other animals) is that you, too, are one of them—a *mammal*.

Rabbits and Relatives

Louis de Lube looked worried. "Boy, am I gonna flunk biology this term," he said to his friend Axel as they worked on a car in the big garage. "I just can't seem to get all that animal classification stuff old Finchley wants us to learn."

"That shouldn't be too tough for a kid who knows as much about cars as you do," said Axel as he wiped grease from his hands.

"Cars make sense, but not all those dumb animals," Louis snorted.

"I wouldn't be so sure about that," said Axel. "The idea behind classifying is the same, whether it's animals, cars, or candy bars. What you do is take a large group of things and break it down into smaller and smaller groups. The smaller the group, the more things are alike.

"Take the cars in this garage—they are all cars, just like animals are all part of the animal kingdom. But do all these cars come from the same part of the world?"

"Naw, you got cars here from all over," said Louis.

"Okay," Axel continued. "Say we put cars from the same part of the world together. The cars from Asia go on the top deck, those from America on the middle deck, and the European cars here on the bottom. That's classifying."

"Yeah, but that's only one step. In my class we gotta put the animals into a lot of smaller groups."

"Let's do it with the cars then. Do all the European cars on this deck come from the same country?"

"Of course not," Louis snapped. "Everyone knows that cars are made in France, Germany, Italy, and other European countries too."

"Then let's divide this deck so that each country gets a separate section for its cars."

"And we could put the cars made by each company in that country in a different aisle," said Louis, catching on to the classification game. "Then we could have a separate bay for each make of car. Like over here, this bay could be only for Volkswagens. All the Volkswagens in the garage would go in this bay, inside this aisle, on this deck."

"You might want to go even further and set aside one row of each bay for each model. You could have one row for Sciroccos, one for Rabbits, and so on," said Axel.

"Hey, if we wanted, we could even have a special space for every type of Rabbit. This one," Louis said with a sweep of his hand, "is reserved only for our Rabbit convertibles."

"See what you did?" asked Axel. "You just figured where all the cars in this garage belong, the Rabbits and all of their relatives." He went over to the message board and made a couple of charts for Louis that showed him how car and animal classification can work. Here's what they looked like:

LOCATION	CLASSIFICATION
GARAGE	ALL CARS
DECK	PART OF THE WORLD
SECTION	COUNTRY
AISLE	COMPANY
BAY	MAKE
ROW	MODEL
SPACE	TYPE

EXAMPLE	ZOOLOGICAL GROUP
ALL CARS	KINGDOM
EUROPEAN	PHYLUM
GERMAN	CLASS
VOLKSWAGENWERKE	ORDER
VOLKSWAGEN	FAMILY
RABBIT	GENUS
CONVERTIBLE	SPECIES

On the right-hand side of the second chart, Axel wrote the classification system zoologists use to group animals. As you look down the chart, you see that the number of animals that belongs in each classification gets smaller and smaller, just as the number of cars in each of Axel's classifications gets smaller as you look down the other side of the chart.

The animal rabbit belongs in the animal kingdom, the phylum Chordata (animals with spinal cords), the class Mammalia (mammals), the order Lagomorpha, the family Laporidae, the genus *Oryctolagus,* and the species *cuniculus.*

Can you use Axel's charts as guides to help you figure out in which groups your family car belongs? If you know cars (and their relatives) pretty well, you will know if your favorite car belongs in the same order as a Buick, the same phylum as a Toyota, or the same class as a Lynx.

What's a Species?

A *species* (SPEE-sees) is a particular kind of plant or animal that is different from others in some important ways. How different and in which ways?

The big difference to zoologists is that only animals that belong to the same species can interbreed and have babies that can themselves later have babies. Each species of animal passes along those things that have made it different from other animals.

That's lucky for us, because we don't have to worry about running into a cross between an elephant and a crocodile—would that be a crocophant?—anywhere except in cartoons, monster movies, or bad jokes.

Each species of animal gets its own two-part name, which is called its scientific name. The first name gives the animal's *genus* (JEAN-us), and the second name its species. That's something like our own first and last names. The genus would be like the last (family) name, and the species name like our own first names—a reverse of the way we use them.

Humans have the scientific name *Homo sapiens* (HO-mo SAY-pee-ens). Like many other scientific names, ours comes from the ancient Latin language; it means "man the wise." Guess which animal made up that name? Right!

You Name It!

Scientific names are not only interesting, they can be very funny. The names that some poor animals got stuck with make you wonder about the people who named them in the first place.

Here are two lists: one is tongue-twisting scientific names and the other is a mixed-up list of the common names of the same animals. Can you match them correctly?

YOU NAME iT!!

1. SUS SCROFA
2. TORPEDO NOBILIANA
3. PHOENICOPTERUS RUBER
4. HIPPOSPONGIA EQUINA
5. MUS MUSCULUS
6. BOS TAURUS
7. BITIS ARIETANS
8. FELIS DOMESTICUS
9. RANA CATESBEIANA
10. RHINOLOPHUS HIPPOSIDEROS
11. CANIS LUPUS
12. PAN TROGLODYTES

a. BATH SPONGE
b. BULLFROG
c. HORSESHOE BAT
d. CATTLE
e. CHIMPANZEE
f. ELECTRIC RAY
g. WOLF
h. HOUSE MOUSE
i. CAT
j. PIG
k. PUFF ADDER (SNAKE)
l. FLAMINGO

ANSWERS!

1-j. If you are looking a little piggy, someone might say you are "scruffy" looking. 2-f. The electric ray (cousin of sharks and stingrays) can carry up to 220 volts of electricity, making it a "noble torpedo." 3-l. This sounds like the name of a bouncing helicopter, but it's actually the name of a long-legged bird, the flamingo. (The species name *ruber* actually means "red" and refers to the pinkish color flamingos often have.) 4-a. The common bath sponge looks like a plant but is really a sea animal. 5-h. With a name like *musculus*, you might expect a big, strong animal. Instead, you get a tiny mouse. 6-d. If you know about the signs of the zodiac, you might have recognized *taurus*, the "bull." Or you might have thought of Bossie the cow. 7-k. Here's a name that makes some sense. *Bitis* is just what you wouldn't want this very poisonous snake to do! 8-i. *Felis* is the genus of some small animals, such as our domestic cat (*Felis domesticus*), and some not-so-small ones, such as the cougar, or mountain lion (*Felis concolor*). 9-b. This animal makes a noise something like its name. Try saying "rana, rana, rana" and hear for yourself. 10-c. Part hippo and part rhino? Nope, this one is all bat. 11-g. The members of the canine genus (*Canis*), much like the feline genus (*Felis*), include both wild and tame animals. The wolf (*lupus*) has some close relatives in the dog (*C. domesticus*) and the fox. 12-e. The *Pan* in this case came from the name of a funny-looking guy in mythology who ran around in the woods playing his panpipes. Chimps don't do this, but they do hang out in forests.

Going Ape

Most people think of apes as big monkeys. Scary ones, at that. Remember King Kong, the giant ape in the movies? He got loose in the big city and went around crushing cars as if they were so many aluminum cans, climbing hundred-story buildings, and swatting airplanes as if they were flies.

You may also have noticed that a lot of bad guys on Saturday morning cartoon shows look very apelike. That's really too bad, because our closest relatives are really nothing like those mean, destructive ape-creatures you see in the movies and on TV.

Our closest relatives? Those hairy apes? Of all the animals in the world, the apes are our nearest kin. In fact, a zoologist would tell you it's more correct to call a human an ape than to say that an ape is a monkey. We are every bit as monkeylike as our ape cousins.

If you look beneath that hairy exterior, you'll see that apes are very different from monkeys in many ways.

Monkeys are *quadrupedal,* that is, they walk around on four legs; apes are designed to be mostly *bipedal* (two

MONKEYS ARE QUADRUPEDAL.

APES HAVE VERTICAL DIGESTIVE SYSTEMS.

APES ARE BIPEDAL.

MONKEYS HAVE HORIZONTAL DIGESTIVE SYSTEMS.

legs carry most of the load). Monkey digestive systems are arranged like those of dogs and cats, running parallel to the ground. Ape digestive systems have a vertical arrangement that suits their upright posture.

Monkeys have tails, something no ape—gorilla, chimpanzee, orangutan, or gibbon—would be caught having (dead or alive).

Apes have broad shoulders and wide, flat chests, not the narrow, pointed chests monkeys have.

Apes have a peculiar shape to their lower molar teeth that gives them five cusps (crests) instead of the four cusps monkeys have on their molars.

Oh, yes, there is one other animal that shares all of these apelike traits that is not a member of the ape family zoologists call Pongidae. That animal is a member of the same superfamily, called the Hominoidea, and actually has as many hairs covering its body as the apes (but its hairs are much shorter and thinner over most of its body).

You guessed it—the animal is good ol' *Homo sapiens*. Now you have to admit that there is something about a chimp that reminds you of cousin Fred or your kid sister. Check *yourself* out in a mirror with a picture of a real ape.

ACTUAL PHOTO OF COUSIN FRED

17

GIBBON

Lightweight Swingers

Gibbons are the smallest living apes, and the world's greatest acrobats. Full-grown gibbons weigh only around 30 pounds and are less than three feet tall (the bigger variety, the siamangs, are a little larger). These little guys look funny when they walk on the ground because they hold their arms out as if on a tightrope.

But they're at home in the tall trees of the rain forests in Southeast Asia. Gibbons are graceful movers, swinging through the trees faster than you could run on the ground.

All apes are swingers at heart—they are animals that have specialized in getting around by means of *brachiation* (brake-ee-A-shun). Broad chests, long collar bones, and muscular shoulders give them the ability to swing from hand to hand. Only gibbons are small enough to do this very easily when full grown. You can imagine the problems a 500-pound gorilla would have swinging through the trees.

over-hand swings can you make along the branch, or bar, before you have to let go?

You are probably good at brachiation because we humans are very apelike in the way our arms and shoulders work. You may not be impressed with your own swinging ability (especially if you have ever watched a gibbon), but you are a real pro in the trees compared with animals such as dogs or cats.

TWO SWINGERS

YOU'RE NOT TRYING!

How good a brachiator are you? Here are some things you can do to test how gibbonlike you are: Can you hang from a limb, or from a bar at the playground, for ten seconds using both hands? Can you hang for ten seconds using only one hand? How many hand-

Ape for a Day

Before you take a gorilla to school with you, there are a few basic things you should know about your pongid pal. Would you expect a gorilla your age to be taller, shorter, or about the same height as you are? It would be about the same size—gorillas are usually between 5½ and 6½ feet tall when they are full grown at 15 or more years of age.

What about weight? Do you think your gorilla would weigh more or less than you do? No contest here—gorillas are bulky, with a six-foot adult weighing 400 pounds or more. Even a five-foot-tall kid-gorilla may weigh 200 pounds.

But what about brains? Is a gorilla's brain larger, smaller, or about the same size as yours? You and your human classmates have the edge here because a gorilla's brain is about half the size of ours. It is nevertheless one

GORILLA

of the largest brains in the animal kingdom, and nobody should think that your gorilla is stupid.

Here's a tricky one. Do gorillas have more hair, less hair, or about the same number of hairs covering their bodies as you do? You have about the same number of hairs on your body as a gorilla, but yours are shorter and very fine compared to your ape's hair.

What about lunch? What would you feed your ape-schoolmate-for-a-day? Feed it vegetables, lots of them, and plenty of greens. Gorillas in the wild are vegetarians that don't ordinarily eat meat. Because the things they eat are not very nutritious and because they are very large animals, they have to eat piles of the stuff to nourish their large bodies and give them energy.

20

Better plan to bring a large suitcase or two filled with vegies for lunch. Nobody wants to be around a hungry gorilla, and your principal would probably get very upset if your buddy ate the leaves off all the trees around your school.

Otherwise, you should not have much trouble with your gorilla. Despite King Kong's reputation as a destructive brute, most people who have studied gorilla behavior in the wild agree that they are very peaceful animals that never look for trouble. They don't get very much trouble from other animals, of course, because of their size.

Panhandlers

Chimpanzees are the apes most of us know best. These big-eared critters always seem to turn up on TV and in the movies wearing clothing and doing things people do—roller skating, riding bicycles, eating hot dogs, and even driving cars.

Chimps make good actors because they are very much like us. They learn quickly, and their bodies are enough like ours that they can do many of the same things we can (some of them better than we do).

What about chimps in the wild, in the forests of their native Africa? Even there, far away from Hollywood directors, chimps solve problems in very intelligent ways.

CHIMPANZEE

One of the things chimps like to eat is termites. The problem to be solved is that those juicy African termites live inside big nests made of sun-baked mud. Breaking open the whole nest would only make the termites crawl deeper into the ground and escape.

Chimps have figured out a way of getting to the termites. A hungry chimp will take small branches off a nearby tree and carefully strip away all the leaves. Then it makes a small hole in the nest and pokes the stick into the hole until it goes into a termite tunnel. The chimp waits patiently until a termite bites the stick as if it were an intruder. Then the chimp pulls the stick out of the hole without knocking off the termite and, presto, a termite for lunch!

What would you do if you were in the woods without water, and the only water you could find was puddled in small tree hollows? (No cheating by pulling a straw out of your pocket.)

Chimps have been seen solving this problem by making leaf sponges. First the chimp puts a few leaves in its mouth and chews them. This makes the leaves absorbent—that is, they will soak up water. The chimp puts this sponge into the water, then sucks it to get the water.

Which of these things do you think a ten-year-old chimp can do?
1. Throw a rock.
2. Call for help.
3. Learn sign language.
4. Make a sleeping nest.
5. Give its kid brother or sister a ride.
6. Share a bunch of bananas with a friend.
7. Recognize itself in a mirror.
8. Pick up a 200-pound weight.
9. Hang by its tail.

A *Pan troglodyte* can do all these things except one—it can't hang by its tail, since it doesn't have one. Chimps may look cute on TV, but full-grown ones (ten years old or older) are nothing to play around with. They weigh a hundred pounds or more and are stronger than a man three times their weight.

Feet with Fingers!

Question: What animal can feed itself a piece of fruit, pick another one, hold onto a tree, and scratch its head at the same time? Answer: The orangutan, a cinnamon-colored ape that has very talented toes. So talented, in fact,

CHIMPANZEE CAUGHT CHEATING WITH A STRAW

ORANGUTAN

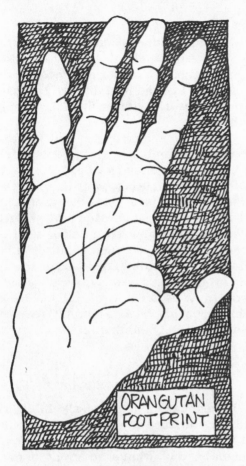

ORANGUTAN FOOT PRINT

Our feet are different, but we can do several other things with them besides walking.

1. See if you can pick up and throw a rock with your feet.

2. Try to pick up a pencil with your toes.

3. Find out how well you can write your name when you hold the pencil between your toes.

4. Try to eat a carrot or a piece of celery using only your feet.

How good are the fingers on your feet?

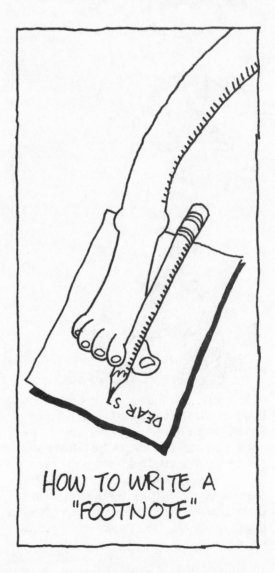

HOW TO WRITE A "FOOTNOTE"

that it can do practically anything with its feet that it can do with its hands.

Orangutans are difficult animals to find except in zoos, where most of them live today. Their original homeland is the forest of Southeast Asia on the big islands of Borneo and Sumatra. The name *orangutan* means "old man of the woods," a pretty good description of this shy ape. Despite the fact that adults are usually four to five feet tall and weigh a hundred pounds or more, orangs live most of their lives in the trees. That's why they need those ex-tra-handy feet. Orang feet look very much like orang hands, with four long toes that work like fingers and a stubby big toe that acts as a thumb. The heavy orangs use all four "hands" as they move slowly through the trees, and even stop once in a while to hang up-side down by their feet.

Hands Down

Apes are among the largest and most intelligent creatures on earth. But it is the apes' close cousin—the one who walks around on two legs all the time—who wins the most unusual animal contest hands down.

Actually, it's the walking around on two legs all the time that makes us different from our close relatives the apes. Our feet are so good at doing the job of getting us from place to place that we don't need to use our hands for that purpose (apes sometimes use their knuckles for balance when they stand or walk). Our hands are free to do other things.

Human hands are made so that there are a lot of other things they can do. Our thumbs are longer and more flexible than ape thumbs, and we can use them to work with each of our four fingers.

To get some idea of just how important your thumb is in all the wonderful things your hands can do, keep your thumb tucked next to your palm while you try to: pour a glass of water and drink it, bounce and catch a large ball with one hand, sweep the floor with a broom, brush your teeth, button and unbutton something, tie a shoelace.

If you are very good with your hands, you may be able to do all of these things, but you have to admit it's easier with the trusty old thumb.

How You Rate as a Primate

If you can hold this book in your hands and turn the pages with your fingers, you are a primate. So what's a primate, and what's so great about being one? Following are some clues.

The first three grades in school are called the "primary" grades. People sometimes call things they consider the best of their kind "primo." The head of most governments is called the "prime" minister, and the hours in the evening when the greatest number of people watch TV are labeled "prime" time.

Get the idea? A primate is a member of a very special group of animals—the number one group, you might say. It stands to reason that the boastful animal who decided to call this group Number One in the Animal Kingdom also included itself. That's just what we humans have done.

The primates include not only man and our close relatives the apes, but a wide variety of monkeys and monkey-like creatures. One important feature all primates share is that they are good grabbers—we have grasping hands.

Think of it this way. If you give a dog or cat (or nearly any other mammal) something good to eat, the animal takes the food from you with its teeth. But a primate will reach out its hand instead, and give the morsel a close looking-over before eating it. Nonprimates are more likely to sniff than to look at their food. Primates use their hands and eyes where other animals rely on their teeth and noses.

Monkey See . . .

Primates have very good vision compared with most other animals' sight. In fact, we have two very special visual abilities. One is the ability to see in three dimensions, which allows us to judge distances very accurately. Animals that don't have three-dimensional vision use a lot of guesswork.

See for yourself how this works. Find a glass or some other small container and put it on a table in front of you. Sit or stand so that your eyes are about level with the top of the glass.

Now cover one of your eyes (or close one eye so that you can't see anything out of it). Using the other eye, try to put your finger into the middle of the glass without touching the sides.

Tougher than you thought? It's easy with both eyes open, because seeing things with both eyes at the same time lets you judge distances *stereoscopically*. (That means seeing double—in stereo—just as you hear *stereophonically* when sound reaches both your ears.)

If the glass trick is too easy for you, try this. Place a small coin on the table, rest your chin on the tabletop, and see if you can put your finger directly on the coin while using only one eye. Then have your friends try it. They'll be surprised how hard it is to touch the coin without a lot of practice.

A World of Colors

The other unusual characteristic that primates have is the ability to see in color. Most other animals don't see things in color the way we do. For them the world is like watching a black-and-white TV.

Having color vision allows us to see a number of details we would miss if we could only see in black and white. An easy way to see how this works is to put a black-and-white and color TV next to each other and notice the things you *don't* see on the black-and-white set.

The world isn't just a TV screen. Here's another way to understand how many animals see. Find some colored lenses to look through. These may be colored plastic toys that you can see through, or colored see-through candy wrappers. They will imitate black-and-white lenses best if you put two of them together (red and green probably will work best).

Now take a look in your refrigerator. Can you tell the difference between green and red apples? What about oranges? Or look at jellybeans or another multicolored candy. You probably have your own favorite flavors, which have their own special colors. Can you pick them out looking through your black-and-white filter?

Of course, primates don't use their color vision just to pick out jellybeans they like, but it does help them find food. When they find it, color vision lets them know whether or not it is ripe and ready to eat—something very important to fruit-loving primates. If you have ever gone out on a limb to pick an unripe apple, or eaten a blackberry that's still red, you know just how important good color vision can be.

Anyone for a lime green banana?

MOST ANIMALS DON'T SEE IN COLOR...

CHAPTER TWO
OUT ON A LIMB

Biologically speaking, we humans are new kids on the block. If you could go back in time only one-hundredth (1/100) of Earth's history, you wouldn't find any human animals walking around on the planet when you got there. At that time, our particular branch of the tree of life was nothing more than a tiny bud.

Today we are out on a limb — the only surviving member of the family Hominidae. For something like the past 20 million (20,000,000) years, we have been slowly and gradually changing from the promising animal we once were into human beings.

But that doesn't mean that we are orphans without ancestors. We have looked into our past and discovered that the hominids who came along before us were very interesting creatures in their own right.

So let's have a look at 'em.

The Family Genes

Sometimes adults say things such as "You look just like your daddy," or

"Aren't you the spitting image of your mother?" Annoying as that may seem —you know you look exactly like yourself and nobody else—you have to admit that parents often do look like their children. They ought to, because parents pass on their *genes* to children. These genes (pronounced like the jeans you wear) are tiny chemical messengers inside every living creature. They control the way a critter grows and develops, and they make sure that it turns out to be very much like its parents.

Take a collie puppy, for instance. If it has a collie mother and father, the genes it got from each of them make sure that it grows a long, shiny coat and that well-known collie needle-nose. The same thing happens with beavers, whose flat tails are passed on to (or you could say are *inherited* by) each new generation of beavers.

What things have you inherited from your parents and your parents' parents? Did you get a distinctive "family" nose, ears, or chin? You can do a little investigation into your own genes by asking some questions and making a family tree.

Start with a good-size piece of paper turned lengthwise so that it is wider than it is tall. Then put yourself in the picture. In the middle of the paper, near the lower edge, make a small square if you are a boy, a small circle if you are a girl. Beside your symbol, draw other ones to represent your brothers and sisters, if you have any. Use a circle for girls, a square for boys.

If you are a boy who has a brother and two sisters, the bottom line of your family tree will look like this:

That takes care of your generation, so you can move up to the next—your parents. First, draw a vertical line from the one you and your brothers and sisters are on and make a double line across to connect your mother and father.

Here's what a family with two children might look like:

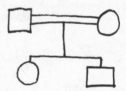

Don't stop there. Your parents probably have brothers and sisters, too, and you will want to include your grandparents and their generation above your parents. Beneath each circle or square, write the person's name and year of birth (especially if you are interested in figuring out ages).

You may want to include other information on your family tree. How tall are the people in your family? The height you and your sisters and brothers will be when you are grown is something you may be able to guess by looking at the height of adult members of your family. Underneath each symbol, name, and year of birth, write the height of each relative on your chart.

There may be other things you'll want to find out about your family and write down on the tree. You can use crayons or colored pencils to add things such as hair color, eye color, whether someone was left-handed, or became bald.

Some of the things that interest you most may not be easy to find out—who is old enough to remember what color great-aunt Lizzie's eyes were, or how tall your great-great-grandfather was?

Here's an example of a family tree and some of the things you may want to include in yours:

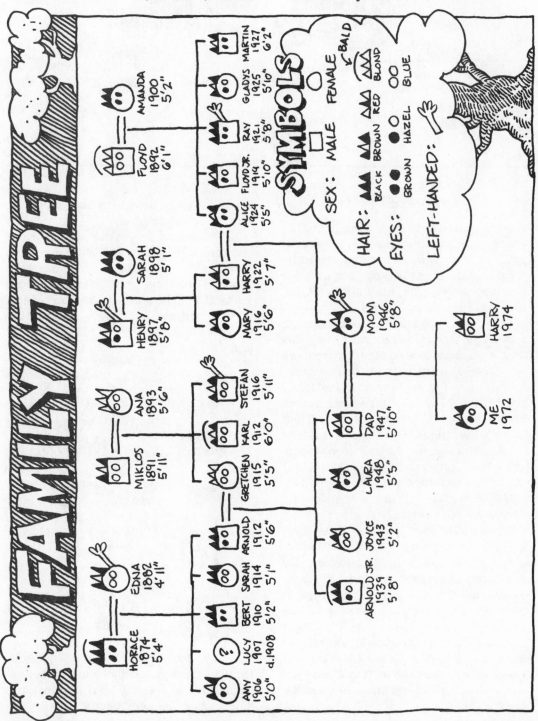

A Peek at the Past

With some help you can probably trace your family tree back several generations without much trouble. Your grandparents, or even your great-grandparents, may still be alive today to help you.

But what if you want to go back much farther, to find out what your very distant ancestors looked like? There are no photos of them in the family album, so you have to use your imagination.

Try this. Draw a picture of an ancestor who lived 10,000 years ago. Then draw other ones from even farther back in time. Keep adding zeros to the age of each one so that you make drawings for ancestors who lived 100,000, 1,000,000, 10,000,000, and even as long as 100,000,000 years ago.

Before you start on your drawings, there is something you should know about genes. They don't stay exactly the same over long periods of time. Small changes take place from time to time in the chemical messages the genes carry, and these small changes can add up over hundreds of generations. If we take a peek at the distant past, we see how those small changes have added up to very big ones over the years.

See if your drawings are anything like these descriptions:

10,000 years ago: Your ancestors of ten thousand years ago were so much like you that you could dress them up in modern clothes and nobody would know the difference. More important, even a medical doctor wouldn't be able to notice any differences between them and you.

100,000 years ago: One hundred thousand years ago people were different than they are today. From the neck down they looked pretty much the same, but their heads did not. Their foreheads were not as high as ours, and their chins didn't stick out as far, but their brains were just as large and they probably were as smart as people today.

1,000,000 years ago: No matter how you dressed up your ancestors of one million years ago, they would stand out in a crowd today. They were smaller than most of us (five-footers were tall people a million years ago!). But the most noticeable difference between them and you is the face. They had heavy eyebrow ridges, sloping foreheads, and, for all we know, their hair may have grown right down to their eyebrows. Their lower jaws were big, with large molar teeth, but they didn't have chins that stick out the way ours do today. These ancestors had brains that were smaller than ours. Even with all these differences, a drawing of your relatives of a million years ago would look a lot like you if you drew only their bodies.

10,000,000 years ago: Your ancestors of ten million years ago might be hard to recognize. They were little, standing only about three feet tall and weighing 50 pounds or so when fully grown. They had no forehead or chin, a much smaller brain, and a huge jaw, but there were still things about them that show a family resemblance: they walked around on two legs the way we do, and their hands looked pretty much like ours.

What did their hair, skin, and eyes look like? Nobody really knows. You could have drawn them with long hairy coats.

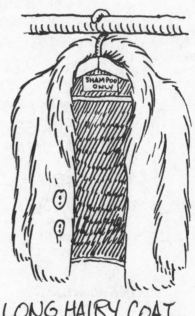

LONG HAIRY COAT

100,000,000 years ago: If you could travel back in time, you would have to look very carefully to find your relatives from a hundred million years ago, and it would be understandable if you didn't recognize them when you saw them.

They were very small, probably had furry coats, and ran around on all fours. You might mistake them for ground squirrels or even for some kind of rat, but if you took a close look, you would notice that their teeth and hands (paws?) didn't look like those of any animal living today.

If you draw in some background, you will want to picture your distant relatives carefully climbing around in the trees and bushes where they lived. It was the heyday of the dinosaurs.

The Evolution Game

It may be hard to believe that a bunch of barely noticeable changes could have turned a ratty-looking little mammal into a large, upright primate in only a hundred million years. From what we know today, however, it looks as if that slow gradual process is exactly how all living things got to be the way they are.

Evolution is the word we use to name the never-ending process of change in living things. Animal life on Earth began about 2½ billion (2,500,000,000)

years ago. The first simple animals started out as one species with genes that were very much alike.

Once in a while there were slight changes in the genes of some animals. Most of the changes were more harm than help in the business of living, but every now and then the slight changes gave an animal a little better chance of living successfully and having offspring than others.

Over very long periods of time, those tiny changes added up to much larger ones. So now there were groups of animals that were not much like their distant ancestors or their living cousins. Very distant cousins are just what such creatures as jellyfish, flatworms, insects, frogs, and humans really are today. We all trace our beginnings back to the earliest living animals.

You can get some idea of how changes like this happen by playing the Evolution Game. All you need is one die (one-half of a pair of dice) to roll and the game board on page 36.

To play the Evolution Game, you start as a simple, one-cell animal, too small to be seen without a microscope. Then, with each roll of the die, you change your genes. Will you ever make it to be a human, a baboon, or even a bat?

Your first roll decides whether you even survive. If you get a 2, 4, or 6, you are on your way to being a more complicated animal. But if you roll a 1, 3, or 5, you become *extinct* (that means your kind of animal dies out). Too bad, start over.

If you roll a 2 or 6, you will possibly become a simple, multicell animal. If your first roll is a 2, roll again. If you get a 3, you're a jellyfish and that's all. If you get any other number, you're extinct.

The best number to roll the first time is a 4. That is the evolutionary step to the higher animals. But even then, if you don't roll a 5 on your second try, you become extinct too.

Try it a bunch of times and see how far you can get up the evolutionary ladder. If you become extinct most of the time, don't be surprised—most of the animals that ever lived have had the same fate. In fact, the trickiness of rolling the right numbers will give you some idea of how hard it is for a species to survive.

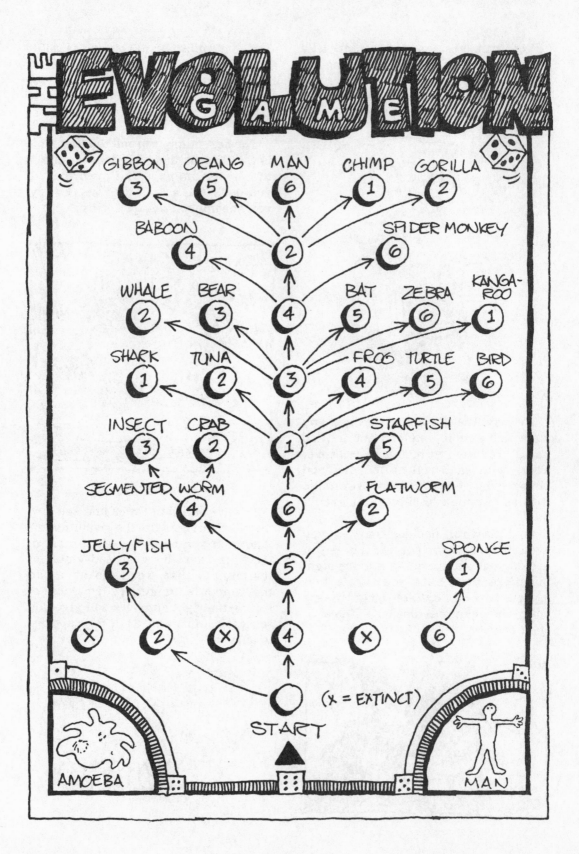

Did you ever make it up to the number 1 on the fourth roll? If you didn't, try it from there now. Now you can end up as anything from a shark to a bird; you will be some kind of *vertebrate* (an animal with a backbone) at this stage of evolution. If you roll a 3, you go on to another level—the mammals.

Only if you roll a 4 after that are you a primate. You may end up a baboon or a spider monkey on your next roll (or extinct if you roll a 1, 3, or 5), but look how far you've come. If you happen to roll a 2, you are in the select company of the living apes and humans. A 6 on the final roll and you become *Homo sapiens*.

Notice that you don't go through the step of being an ape before you become a human. In evolutionary terms the 2 on the next to last level is neither ape nor man. It's just a common ancestor we shared in the past, a player who left the scene millions of years ago.

If this game seems to take too long to play, with all those dead ends of extinction, remember how long it took the animals to do it in real life. The starting spot is where our most ancient ancestors were about 2½ billion years ago.

Ruler of Time

One of the most important ingredients in evolution is time. People who have a hard time believing that animals have changed from microscopic one-cell animals into whales and elephants need to be reminded that it didn't happen overnight.

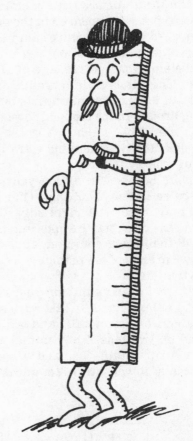

You can get some idea of the vast amounts of time involved by measuring them with a ruler. One of the colored plastic kind will do just fine, or any other one that is twelve inches (one foot) long.

The left edge of your ruler is the time of Earth's origin, believed to have been about 4½ billion years ago (written in numeral form, that's 4,500,000,000).

If you use your ruler to mark evolutionary events that have happened since then, here's where they would be on your ruler of time:

2½ inches: 3½ billion years ago, the first forms of life appeared on Earth.

5¼ inches: 2½ billion years ago, the first animals appeared. Earth was already 2 billion years old.

10½ inches: 500 million (½ billion) years before the present was about the time the first animals with backbones (the vertebrates) appeared in the seas. These were the first fishlike animals.

11½ inches: 200 million years ago was the early part of the Age of Dinosaurs. The first little animals that could call themselves mammals began poking around in the tropical forests of that time. The mighty Himalayas, Alps, and Rocky Mountains were then just low rolling plains.

11 15/16 inches: 20 million years on your ruler is only 1/16 inch (the last small mark) from the right edge. This is about the time that the apes and man shared their last common ancestor. Our own branch of the primates was on its own at last.

11 99/100 inches: 4 million years ago a small animal lived in east Africa. It was about four feet tall, and walked around on two legs. This animal was called Australopithecus, and at least one form of it was our direct ancestor.

11 199,999/200,000 inches: 2,000 years ago was when people began using our modern system of numbering years. Nearly one hundred generations of humans have lived since that time—a lot of people, but a speck of time. It would take a good microscope to see the part of your ruler 2,000 years represents. About 10,000 spaces this size would fit between the last 1/16 mark and the end of the ruler! The sizes we are thinking about here are so small that they are hard to see. By using the 3,028 miles between Washington, D.C., and San Francisco, California, as your ruler, you can get a better idea. The last 2½ miles of that distance can represent the last four million years of our evolution. Then the last seven feet one inch (the height of a tall basketball player)

EARTH BEGINS— 4½ BILLION YEARS AGO

FIRST LIFE FORMS APPEAR — 3½ BILLION YEARS AGO

FIRST ANIMALS— 2½ BILLION YEARS AGO

represents the 2,000 years since we began numbering our years.

It's an old, old world we live in. So the next time you are 30 seconds late for school, calmly ask your teacher not to get so excited about it. After all, it took the human species nearly all of Earth's 4½ billion years to get here.

Stones and Bones

Since we're all curious about our beginnings, it's lucky for us that we have fossil ancestors to give us some idea of what early humans were like. (*Fossils* are parts or imprints of once-living things that have become mineralized, or turned to stone, after being buried in the ground for thousands of years or more.)

Unfortunately, there are not many human fossils, and they are very difficult to find. Take a relative of ours from two million years ago, for instance. How does it get to be a fossil we can find and recognize? It isn't easy.

First of all, our ancestor has to die in the right place. Bone usually decomposes (breaks up) and becomes part of the soil. Or the body gets moved, and the bones are scattered. But if conditions are just right, the bones slowly fossilize.

A LOT OF STUFF HAPPENED IN THAT LAST 1/16 INCH...

WHO'S THIS NEWCOMER?

WE FINALLY MADE IT!

STOP SHOVING.

11 15/16 INCHES

FIRST DINOSAURS— 200 MILLION YEARS AGO

FIRST VERTEBRATES— 500 MILLION YEARS AGO

WHERE WE ARE TODAY

In time our fossil ancestor gets buried deeper and deeper in the ground. Have you ever noticed the way dust accumulates on shoes you don't often wear? Then you have some idea of how much dust could collect if you left the shoes outside for a couple million years.

After two million years our fossil might be buried under 10, 20, or even 100 feet of soil. That means a lot of digging to find it today. Luckily there are places where wind and water have done much of the hard work of digging for us. The Grand Canyon of the Colorado River in North America is such a place; the mighty river has cut through millions of years of soil and soft rock like a knife through a chocolate layer cake. The deeper you go down the walls of the canyon, the farther you are going back in time.

The people who find fossils have to look very carefully for them, and most often all they find are broken bits and pieces. Some *paleontologists* (pail-ee-un-TAHL-uh-jists) spend many years looking for fossils before they find any.

What they do find wouldn't mean much to anyone but a trained fossil-hunter. The bits and pieces are usually tiny and crushed, sometimes completely stuck to the surrounding rock.

Here's something you can try for yourself the next time your family eats a whole chicken or turkey. Save all of the bones and see how well you can fit the pieces together. You can probably do a pretty good job of putting parts in the right places, but does your recon-

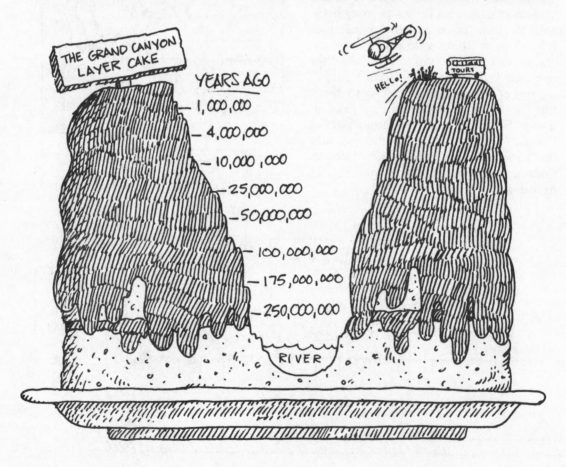

THE GRAND CANYON LAYER CAKE

YEARS AGO
— 1,000,000
— 4,000,000
— 10,000,000
— 25,000,000
— 50,000,000
— 100,000,000
— 175,000,000
— 250,000,000

HELLO!

TOURS

RIVER

struction look very much like the familiar barnyard fowl? This should give you some idea of how difficult it is to imagine what an animal looked like when you have only a few pieces of its bones, and nobody has seen the critter in person for a million years or more.

Toothful Tales

There is an old saying among bad guys in western and gangster movies: "Dead men tell no tales." That's true, but sometimes their teeth do.

Paleontologists often find only teeth when they uncover fossil hominids (our own branch of the primate tree), but they have learned plenty from those durable little chompers. Mammals of the distant past started out with four basic kinds of teeth, and we still have them today. Got a mirror? Take a look at your own.

INCISORS

Those front teeth, the two on each side closest to the middle, are called *incisors*. They are the sharp nippers that you use to cut and tear food—or anything else that happens to wind up in your mouth. Compared with those of our nearest relatives the apes, man has pretty small incisors. We don't use ours nearly as often as apes do to hold and carry things around.

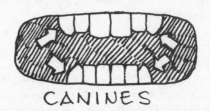

CANINES

That tooth next to your incisor is a *canine*. Notice how it is rounder and more pointed than the ones in front? It gets its name from the genus of animals that includes both dogs and wolves. Their big canine teeth are often called fangs.

We have to stop at this point since the next teeth you see (or don't see) depend on how old you are. Remember those teeth you put under your pillow for the tooth fairy? They were temporary ones called "baby," "milk," or *deciduous* teeth. Besides deciduous incisors and canines, you also have two temporary *molars*. These are designed to do the hard work of grinding food so

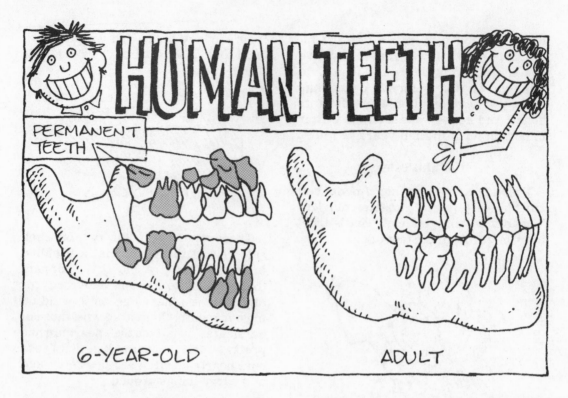

PERMANENT TEETH

6-YEAR-OLD

ADULT

that it can be swallowed and digested more easily.

Do you have any deciduous teeth left? Your temporary incisors should have come out at about 6 or 7 years of age—about the time your first permanent molars came in. Most people lose their deciduous canines and molars between ages 9 and 12.

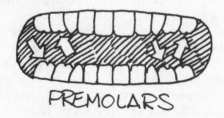

PREMOLARS

The temporary molars are replaced by teeth called *premolars,* and there are two of them. At about the same time this replacement is happening, the second permanent molar comes up from the gums (around 10 to 12 years of age). Do you have yours yet? If not, but

you feel a soreness in your gums behind your first permanent molars, chances are that the second ones are on the way.

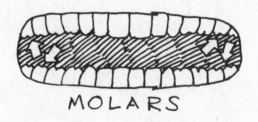

MOLARS

The last molar may be some time in coming. That third permanent molar is sometimes called the "wisdom tooth," because it rarely surfaces before a person is at least 16 years old. Third molars often wait until their owners have reached the ripe old age of 25, or even later. Some people never get them (although that doesn't necessarily mean that they never "wise up").

42

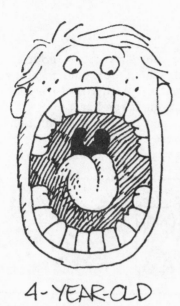

4-YEAR-OLD

What's your dental formula? A four-year-old human's would be written:

$$\frac{2 \cdot 1 \cdot 2}{2 \cdot 1 \cdot 2}$$

This means two incisors, one canine, and two molars per side, all deciduous. (Total: 20 teeth.)

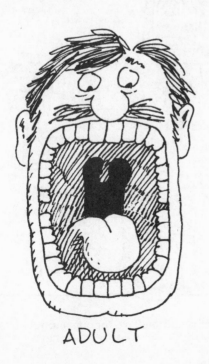

ADULT

The formula for an adult human is

$$\frac{2 \cdot 1 \cdot 2 \cdot 3}{2 \cdot 1 \cdot 2 \cdot 3}$$

with the premolars sneaking in between the canines and molars for a total of 32 teeth.

When they examine fossil teeth closely, paleontologists can determine what the animal's dental formula was, and just how closely the species was related to modern man. The scientists can even tell how old the animal was when it died.

THE SPIRITS TELL ME THIS TOOTH BELONGED TO A GIANT LIZARD WHO WENT BY THE NAME OF BRUCE...

Here are the dental formulas for some other mammals—it's a lot easier to read them here than to go and count them for yourself.

$$\text{PIG:} \quad \frac{3 \cdot 1 \cdot 4 \cdot 3}{3 \cdot 1 \cdot 4 \cdot 3} = 44$$

SPIDER MONKEY: $\dfrac{2.1.3.3}{2.1.3.3} = 36$

CAT: $\dfrac{3.1.3.1}{3.1.2.1} = 30$

RABBIT: $\dfrac{2.0.3.3}{1.0.2.3} = 28$

BABOON: $\dfrac{2.1.2.3}{2.1.2.3} = 32$

Brain Gain

We humans have gotten swelled heads about our own intelligence, so it's not surprising that we like to brag about our large brains.

Make a raid on your kitchen and dig up these containers from the refrigerator and storage cabinets:

1. **SODA CAN** — 12 oz., OR 355 ml. *

2. **TALL SODA CAN** — ONE PT., OR 16 OZ., OR 473 ml.

3. **WINE OR LIQUOR BOTTLE** — 25.4 OZ., OR 750 ml.

4. **MILK CARTON** — ONE QT., OR 32 OZ., OR 946 ml.

5. **LARGE JUICE CAN** — 46 OZ., OR 1,360 ml.

*Abbreviations: oz. for ounces; ml. for milliliters; pt. for pint; qt. for quart.

What do all these containers represent? Brains!

The small soda can has about the same volume (size, but not shape) as an average chimpanzee brain, and the tall one is about equal to the brain of a gorilla. Our modern ape cousins are very brainy when compared with most animals, but how do they stack up against man and his ancestors?

Around three million years ago, our ancestors had brains about the size of the modern gorilla's. But these little guys were much smaller than today's ape, so we can assume they were probably a bit smarter than gorillas.

As man evolved over the next 1½ million years, that brain got larger. By then, the ancestral brain would have filled that wine or liquor bottle—750 milliliters or perhaps a little more.

Today we have, on the average, slightly smaller brains. Take a look at that big juice can. It represents the volume of brains most of us have today. If you happen to have a larger or smaller head than that, don't feel better or worse than the rest of us. The size of an individual brain doesn't seem to have anything to do with how smart someone is.

Moral: You may have three times the brains of an ape, but no one will notice the difference if you just sit on your can.

By one million years ago, our direct ancestors had grown brains as large as the quart milk carton.

But *Homo sapiens* didn't stop there. The brain kept right on getting larger until it reached an average size equal to two of those wine bottles—1,500 milliliters. (You might have one of those big 1½-liter wine bottles around your house. That's the same size.) At least, that is the size of the brains of some of our ancestors of 100,000 years or so ago.

Fossil Hall of Fame

There are bubble gum cards for nearly everything these days. Why not some for our prehistoric ancestors?

Open a pack of Rubble-Bubble Fossil Gum and here are some of the facts you would be likely to find on the backs of the cards. You get to draw the faces on the front yourself. Remember that fossils lack skin, hair, and eyeballs, so you don't have to draw anything but their skulls.

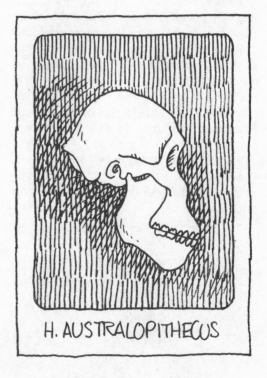

Homo australopithecus: "Southern ape man." Height: 4 feet 4 inches. Weight: 80 pounds. Age: 2 million years.

Australopithecines seem to have lived only in Africa, and came in a wide variety of sizes and shapes during the three million or so years they were part of the evolutionary first string.

They were little guys with small braincases and very large jaws with big teeth in them. Their incisors were especially large compared to later ones. You might be able to beat them in a spelling bee, but you wouldn't want to challenge them to a pie-eating contest.

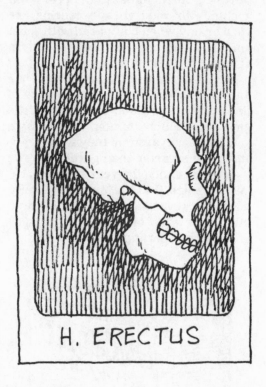

Homo erectus: "Pithecanthropus," "Peking man," "Java man." Height: 5 feet. Weight: 120 pounds. Age: 800,000 years.

These stocky people lived through the early part of the Ice Age, and are often said to have been the first to use fire regularly. They had long, low braincases, larger than those of the australopithecus. Their brow ridges were very thick and heavy, and they didn't have much forehead. Jaws were still large, but much less massive than australopithecus jaws.

These guys would make great hockey players—low to the ice, and they would not need helmets to protect their skulls.

had, but the big Neanderthal jaws could do some serious chewing. Some football coaches wish they had one or two of these hefty guys to play fullback or linebacker.

Homo sapiens: "Modern man."
Height: 5 feet 8 inches. Weight: 145 pounds. Age: 25,000 years.

This newcomer to the hominid line is the first ancestor who could play forward on a basketball team. The tiny jaw with a stuck-out chin and small teeth, and a large, rounded braincase with a forehead make this animal look strange to the other fossils in the hall. Our fossil ancestors would consider this skinny-looking creature with the bubble head a real lightweight.

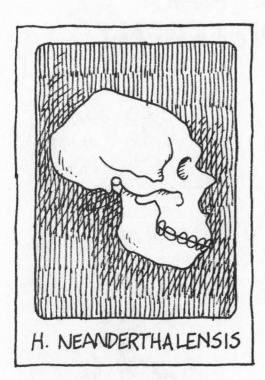

H. NEANDERTHALENSIS

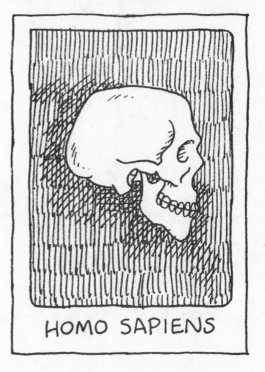

HOMO SAPIENS

Homo neanderthalensis: "Neanderthal man," "cave man." Height: 5 feet 3 inches. Weight: 160 pounds. Age: 60,000 years.

Some people think of Neanderthal man as a stupid, shaggy cave dweller who sat around grunting and gnawing on bones. Don't let him hear you say that!

The Neanderthal people actually had larger brains than we do, inside a long, low, and narrow braincase. They had big eye sockets, with brow ridges almost as heavy as those of the pithecanthropus. There wasn't much more of a chin than the earlier people had

FASCINATING STUFF!

CHAPTER THREE
ALIKE IS DIFFERENT

MY NAME'S TARZAN, I WEIGH 43 POUNDS, I LOVE LIVER, SLEEPING, PLAYING "FETCH", AND LICKING THE MAILMAN...

MY NAME'S JANE. I WEIGH 44 POUNDS, I LOVE FRENCH FRIES, BARKING, GARBAGE CANS, AND CHASING THE MAILMAN...

When you see a Chihuahua and a Saint Bernard together, you wonder how in the world they could be members of the same species of animal. And yet they are both dogs (*Canis domesticus*).

The fact is that no two bath sponges, horseshoe bats, boa constrictors, or human beings look exactly alike, even if they are members of the same individual species. That's because genes (remember those little bits of hereditary material we pass on from *gene*ration to generation) are not perfect cookie cutters. They make sure all members of a species are the same in general design, but they allow quite a bit of individual variation.

This helps explain why you don't look just like your brothers and sisters. What it doesn't explain completely is why Saint Bernards and Chihuahuas look so different, or why people who live in different parts of the world have different heights and body builds.

If you're interested in these differences, where they came from, and what they mean, read on.

Out of the Pool

You'll get an idea of how a single species can have groups that are different from each other if you try this experiment. Get a large container that will hold at least a quart of water (two quarts would be even better), a small glass, and a thermometer. The thermometer should be the kind that measures outside temperatures, not the kind that you put in your mouth when you think you are sick with a fever.

Fill the large container with water. Now the drops of water in your container represent all the genes belonging to a particular species of animal. All together, they make up that animal's *gene pool*.

JEAN POOL
NOT TO BE CONFUSED WITH A "GENE POOL"

In real life it sometimes happens that a group of animals becomes separated from others and becomes isolated. Perhaps the small group moved into a new territory, or found itself cut off from other members of its species by some barrier, such as the changed course of a river or a lack of food in the area around it.

To find out what might happen in a case like that, take a small group of genes (drops of water) out of the pool (the whole container of water). Isolate them (fill the small glass with water from the large container). The temperature of the water in both containers should be about the same, just as you would expect the genes of both groups to be about the same. But what if conditions change for the small group?

Change them in your isolated group by putting the small glass into your freezer (or another part of your refrigerator if there isn't enough room in the freezer) for ten minutes.

When the ten minutes are up, take the glass out of the freezer and take the temperature of the water inside. How much did it change? Now measure the temperature of the large container again (it may have changed a little too).

If you hadn't taken the glass out of the freezer after ten minutes, the water in it would have continued to get colder until it turned into ice. That's something like what happens to isolated groups cut off from the larger pool. The small group may be faced with changing conditions, and its genes slowly change in response. At this point you might call the drops in the small glass a "race" of water. Given enough time, they may develop enough differences so that they become a separate species of animal.

For now, let's say that the isolation ends before the small group changes that much. Pour the water from the small glass back into the large container and measure the temperature of the mixture. Notice that it is closer to the temperature of the water left in the large container than it is to the temperature of the water in the small glass. Genes act this way too—describing a gene pool is mostly a counting game.

The changes that took place in the small group are important because they have contributed new genes to the whole pool, or at least altered its make-up a little.

Dealing Differences

Another thing that can bring about group variation within a species is chance. This can happen whenever a small group splits off from the larger population.

Here's how it works. Get a deck of playing cards. There should be 52 cards in the deck, not counting the jokers. Make sure the cards are well shuffled, and then deal yourself five of them.

Now take a look at the five cards you have dealt. Let's say that the suits (clubs, diamonds, spades, and hearts) are the genes that control height in a population, going from the tallest (clubs) down through the shortest (hearts). Are your five cards taller or shorter than the rest of the "population"?

Simply by chance you may have gotten more clubs and diamonds than spades and hearts, making your small group taller than the remaining population. The differences may be slight, or they could be great.

In the same way, when a small group becomes isolated from the rest of the population, it may have more tall genes. Even if there are no evolutionary pressures causing tallness to be of some advantage, this small group is different from the rest.

HOW THE LeNODS GOT THEIR SPOTS

"Uncle Ham, we want to know how come there are so many different-looking kinds of LeNods," said Mary one afternoon. Ham looked up from his *LeNod Times* and saw his nieces and nephews gathered around him in his bazooma-tree home.

Back to your five cards again. Let's suppose the number of the card determines hair color. For example, we'll make the numeral cards 2 to 10 the genes for black hair, jacks for blond hair, queens for red hair, aces and kings for brown hair.

You may have drawn two queens among your five cards. In that case, your isolated population is *very* different from the remaining group. The big bunch now has only two redheads among 47 members, while your group has two of them out of only 5.

Chance in this case has led to a gene difference between the two groups far greater than you would expect.

"Okay, kids, here's the story. At one time, all of us LeNods were a solid golden color."

51

"That can't be true," said Barry. "I've never seen a golden LeNod, and I never heard of one."

"Nevertheless it's true," continued Uncle Ham. "That's the way our ancestors looked when they used to live on the ground. But then some of them found out that they could get more food, and much more easily, if they gathered bazooma nuts on the tree instead of waiting until the nuts fell to the ground.

"For a while things were just great, and our golden-furred ancestors multiplied pretty fast. But then it happened —the wampuza birds that lived in the forests began to prey more and more on LeNods."

"Wampuzas!" shivered Sherry, her whiskers twitching with fear.

"They did, and there got to be fewer and fewer LeNods in the forest. But there were a few LeNods—there always had been—who had different colors from the rest. Out in the grasslands, these were the ones who usually got eaten first. A brown LeNod was easy for predators to see.

"But in the forests, a brown LeNod was difficult for the wampuzas to see. So more and more of the brown LeNods survived, and most of their children were brown."

"About that time, a group of LeNods that had been living on the edge of the bazooma forests made a new discovery. They discovered that podunk trees have seeds that are good to eat. The only trouble was that the podunk seeds had much harder shells than the bazoomas and there were not many of them to be found in the bazooma forest.

"This little group of LeNods wandered into the land where the podunk trees were more numerous, and there was more to eat. Those among them that had the larger and stronger teeth got more to eat, and the ones with average or small teeth didn't do so well. After a few generations, these LeNods had bigger teeth than the group that was still living in the bazooma forest."

couldn't find enough LeNods to feed themselves. Some of them who were searching for food at the edge of the forest began finding LeNods in the podunk trees. Those LeNods were sitting ducks with their brown coats against the gray-speckled bark of the podunks. So the wampuzas caused the brown-coat LeNods to get fewer and fewer in number.

"Okay, that's why some LeNods have big teeth, but how did they get their spots? You haven't said anything about that yet, Uncle Ham," said Larry.

"I was just coming to that part," he answered. "It just so happened that the wampuzas were having a hard time back there in the bazooma forest. They

"Now there had always been some LeNods that had grayish coats, and these did a lot better than the others

living among the podunk trees. But they still had a difficult time because even the stupid wampuzas could see their solid gray coats against the speckled bark of the podunks. That's when the few LeNods that had spots on their coats—they used to be called 'blotchers,' and everyone thought they were ugly—found that they had an advantage. Wampuzas couldn't see them against the podunk bark, and soon there were more of them than any other kind of LeNod in the podunk areas.

a few blotchers out in the grasslands among our golden cousins.

"I guess the thing you all should remember is that it's lucky for us that there were some differences among LeNods in the past. And no matter what we look like, we are all real LeNods under the fur.''

BLOTCHED LE NOD IN FRONT OF PODUNK TREE

"So that's why today there are three varieties, or races, of LeNods—gray ones with spots and big teeth, brown ones with small teeth, and even some golden ones, which you've never seen, living in the grasslands. But that isn't the whole story.

"There are still some grayish LeNods living in the bazooma forest, and

Tell-Tale Tails

"Gladys, am I ever happy to see you," said Florence as she opened the door to her apartment. There were cats everywhere—cats in chairs, cats on tables, sleeping on the floor, even a cat sitting in the sink.

"What's the matter, Flo, have you had some sort of catastrophe?"

CATS AGAINST BAD CAT JOKES

"I'm really stumped about these two litters of kittens," said Florence. "Just look at the ones with Natalia. They all have tails, and she doesn't have even the hint of a tail herself. Ali's kittens over here," she said pointing to a box with six kittens, "three of them don't have tails even though Ali has a perfectly good one. You don't suppose I mixed them up somehow, do you?"

"Florence, do you know anything about genetics?"

"Sure, I do genetics with the woman on the television every morning."

"No, not 'gymnastics,' Flo, 'genetics,' the study of genes and how they pass traits along from one generation to another. You know, things like why most of the people in your family have curly hair, or why the people on Melvin's side of the family are tall. Genes work the same way for cats."

"Oh yeah? Then how come the mother cat with a tail has some kittens without tails, and the mother cat without a tail ends up with a litter where every kitten has a tail? Can you answer me that one?"

"Well, I learned a few things about genetics from an article I read in *Cat-lover's Digest*. Let me show you how it works," said Gladys, reaching underneath a big tabby cat for a pencil and paper.

"Kittens have a pair of genes for every trait. There are millions of different pairs of genes, which have to do with how long a kitten's fur will grow, what color it will be, how big it gets, and whether or not it has a tail. The pair that has to do with tails is the only one we are going to look at here.

"Now, there are two different kinds of tail genes. The ones that give a cat a tail we'll call a 'T' gene," said Gladys, making a capital T on the paper. "The other kind of gene gives a cat no tail, and we'll call it a 't' gene," she said, making a little t on the paper.

"Where do kittens get the genes?" asked Flo.

"Remember I said that kittens always have genes in pairs? Well, one of the genes each kitten gets comes from the mother cat, and one of them is from the father cat. So what do you think happens when a kitten gets a T gene from the mother and another T from the father cat?"

"I guess you get a kitten with a tail," Flo answered.

CAT WITH PAIR OF "T" GENES

"Right. And if your kitten gets two little t genes?"

"I get a kitten with no tail!" shouted Flo.

CAT WITH PAIR OF "t" GENES

"You've got it." Gladys wrote down these symbols for the two kinds of kittens: TT = tail; tt = no tail.

"Hey, what happens if a kitten gets one T and one t?" Flo asked. "Do I get a kitten with half a tail?"

CAT WITH PAIR OF LEVI JEANS

"Not in this case. A kitten either gets a tail or doesn't get a tail. There isn't an in-between when it comes to tails. What happens here is that one kind of gene is *dominant*. When it is paired with the other kind, the dominant gene wins out. The T gene is the dominant one in this case. If a kitten gets even one T gene, it will have a tail. So your Tt kitten will have a tail that looks just like a TT kitten's tail."

A DOMINANT GENE

"So we can forget about the t in a Tt kitten, right? It doesn't matter."

"Hold on a minute, Flo. Let's look at what happens when your Tt kitten grows up and has kittens of her own. What kind of tails will her kittens have?"

The old cat lady thought it over for a moment, and then answered. "I've got it—half of them will have tails and half of them won't. That must have been what happened with Ali. She has a tail, but only half of her kittens do."

"That's a good guess, Flo. But it doesn't always work out that way. Don't forget that a kitten gets one of those genes from the father cat. How the kittens turn out depends just as much on the kind of genes he has."

Gladys made a drawing that looked something like a tic-tac-toe game on the paper. "We can use this little chart to figure out what kind of kittens we get from mating cats. The top line of the chart shows the two genes from the mother cat. We can put each one in a separate space. The father cat's genes go into the two lower spaces on the left-hand side, one above the other. If we mate a Tt mother cat with a father that has no tail—a tt—here's what our chart looks like.

"All we have to do to figure out what kind of kittens they can have is to add the genes together. Each of the four boxes at the lower right of the chart can be filled in by adding one of the mother's genes from above with one of the father's genes at the left. This gives us the combinations we can get from parent cats that are Tt and tt."

When Flo filled in the chart, here's what she got.

"It looks like I was right. Half of the kittens have tails, and half of them don't," said Flo.

"Partly right. The four boxes of kittens only tell us which combinations of genes are possible. They don't really tell us how many kittens there will be, or how many will be of one kind and how many of another. We expect there will be about half of each kind in this case."

"But what if the father cat was a TT instead? Or what if he was a Tt like our mother cat?"

See if you can help Flo figure out what kind of kittens she would get in each of these two cases.

Tt mother x TT father

All of the kittens would have tails, since each one has at least one dominant T gene. About half of them will be TT kittens, and about half will be Tt with one t, or *recessive* gene. Recessive genes are the opposite of dominant ones. Both genes in a pair have to be recessive for that trait to show.

Tt mother x Tt father

In this case we have three possible types of kitten, TT, Tt, and tt. We can expect that about twice as many of them will be Tt than either TT or tt, but each litter can be different in its exact makeup. Probably, most of the kittens will have tails, since three of our four combinations have the dominant T in them.

What about Flo's tailless cat, Natalia? If all of her kittens had tails, how could she explain this? Can you figure what kind of genes the father must have?

Answer: Since Natalia herself has no tail, she has to be a tt. (That's the only way a recessive trait like taillessness can show up, remember?) She gives each of her kittens one t gene. This means that the only way they can all have tails is if they get a T from the father cat. He has to have a tail; in fact, he almost certainly is a TT. Here is how this chart would look.

tt mother x TT father

In this case, all the kittens have the same gene combination; they are all Tt.

Race and Place

The people who lived in Freetown
All had faces decidedly brown
They just couldn't explain
Why a visiting Dane
Looked as pale as the moon shining
  down.

One answer to the riddle of racial differences and why they exist is found right here in this silly limerick—race is a product of place.

Humans are just like other animals in their need to adapt to environmental conditions where they live. Isolated populations of other animals have produced varieties (or races) of the same species that differ from one another in size, coloration, and other features that are easy to see.

Since humans are a very widespread species (we live in practically every nook and cranny of our planet), it figures that we, too, are a species that shows the effects of geographical isolation.

Take a look at a map of the world (or better yet a globe, if you can find one) and see how some of our planet's great barriers have isolated human populations.

The most impressive barrier that you see is all that blue—the seas and oceans of the world. Until about 500 years ago, these waters were very difficult for large numbers of people to cross, and so they isolated peoples on opposite shores from one another.

Australia and the Americas are good examples of areas that were cut off from the rest of the human population. The people in those places developed some physical differences that have led us to think of them as separate races.

Mountains have played their part in isolating peoples too. Can you find the world's tallest mountain range, the Himalayas? These towering peaks cut the peoples of India off from the other peoples of Asia. The Alps and Carpathians in Europe had somewhat the same effect, for a time separating the peoples of the south from those of northwestern Europe.

Deserts, those dry and barren stretches of land, reduced contact between groups of people to a minimum before the age of modern travel. Can you see how the great Sahara and Libyan deserts isolated the peoples of northern Africa from the rest of that continent? The Gobi desert of eastern

Asia and the Kalahari of southern Africa also acted as barriers between peoples. The separated groups developed different racial characteristics.

Of course, none of these physical barriers was ever high or dry enough to prevent some mixing of people around the fringes. This little bit of contact and the relatively short time that man has been spreading out into the isolated parts of the world have kept the varieties of mankind from becoming separate species.

These old barriers have been lifted by modern travel and the large-scale movements of people during the past 500 or so years. In the streets of most big cities of the world today, you can find people whose ancestors lived in Asia, Africa, Europe, Australia, or the Americas when Columbus made his long voyage between Europe and the Americas.

In our limerick, the people of Freetown, West Africa, and Denmark, northern Europe, represent two populations that were geographically isolated for a long time. Each has developed some unique features, among which skin color is the most visible.

Skin Deep

When people talk about race, they usually are talking about skin color. Color is even used to name races—you hear of the "blacks," "red man," "yellow race," and "whites"—although the people these terms are supposed to describe don't actually have skin of those colors.

Skin colors among the geographic races of mankind do differ. Most people in northwestern Europe, for instance, have skin much lighter than the average residents of Zaire in central Africa.

What makes skin color different from race to race, and how did those color differences come to be? The answer to the first question is *melanin* (MEL-uh-nin). Melanin is a dark substance that is found in grains of different sizes. In every human, just beneath the outer layers of skin, are specialized cells that produce melanin. The more melanin these cells produce, the darker the skin.

All humans have about the same number of melanin-producing cells in their skin. Skin color differs among groups because of differences in their genes. Some populations (races) have genes that direct their cells to produce many large granules of melanin pigment. Others have genes that cause their cells to make only a few smaller granules.

You can see how this works and find out why melanin is important by trying this experiment. Get a clear plastic lid from a storage container, or coffee or

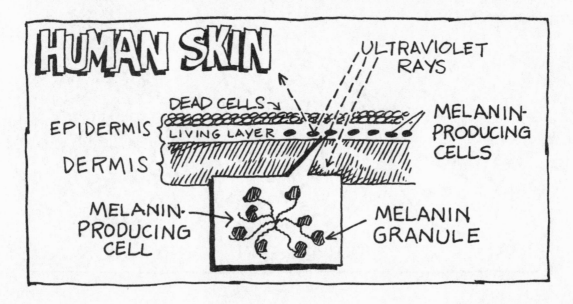

shortening can. Then find some dried beans, peas, or uncooked rice. The only other things you will need are a lamp and a darkened room.

Start by putting a few peas or grains of rice (granules of melanin pigment) on the top of the lid (underlying layer of skin). Hold this under the lamp and notice how much light comes through. The small amount of light blocked by the few grains is similar to the amount of ultraviolet radiation that would be blocked by the melanin produced by light-skinned people.

Ultraviolet radiation is the kind of sunlight that causes sunburn by damaging the skin underneath the melanin layer. (Pain isn't the only thing humans get from ultraviolet radiation. It helps our skin produce vitamin D, which is important in keeping teeth and bones healthy.)

Add some more granules, and you have something like the amount of melanin found in the darker-skinned races. Notice how much of the light is blocked from the areas beneath the lid now— there's less chance of sunburn.

Now put enough grains on the lid so that you lightly cover the whole thing.

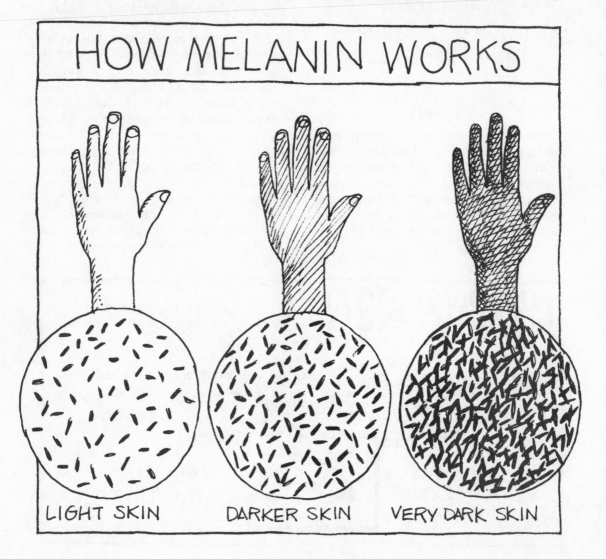

HOW MELANIN WORKS

LIGHT SKIN   DARKER SKIN   VERY DARK SKIN

bers of the "white" race must have had ancestors who lived in areas of the world where the advantage of having ultraviolet radiation reach the lower layers of the skin and help make vitamin D was more important than protection against the sun. The far northern areas of Europe seem to fit these conditions best, and that is where many very light-skinned people still live today.

Back to the Dogs

This is something like what the darkest-skinned humans have in the way of melanin protection. There is still some light that gets through the lid, but much less than before.

One other thing affects the amount of melanin in the skin. The more that skin is exposed to sunlight, the more melanin is produced by the special cells. This extra protection is generally called "tanning," and you have probably noticed how different some people's skin looks in the summer as compared with in the winter.

Check for yourself: how much difference in color do you see between the skin on the back of your hand and the skin on your hip? If you always wear a watch or a ring, you may be able to see a distinct tan line around the skin it covers.

If melanin offers such valuable protection from the burning rays of the sun, doesn't it seem surprising that there are people with light skin? Mem-

Remember our Chihuahua and Saint Bernard? Looking at the differences in their size, shape, color, and coat might lead you to think they are members of different species. But they are both *Canis domesticus*.

Dog breeds got to be as varied as they are today only with the help of man—"human selection," if you like. People have taken over nature's job of deciding which dogs will live and produce puppies. Mates are carefully chosen by owners so that the "pure" characteristics of the particular breed are passed on to future generations, and papers are kept that tell each dog's lineage, or breeding history.

Humans have carefully bred some types of dogs for special characteristics. A few types were bred to be hunters, working with their human masters to catch game. Others have been bred as shepherds, retrievers, guards, or transporters such as sled dogs.

Man has been able to do this kind of artificial selection because of the dog's rapid reproduction rate. One human lifetime may equal thirty or more generations of dogs, and each generation (litter) has several individuals from which a breeder can choose.

Humans have domesticated, or tamed, many other species of animals and controlled their mating in the same ways.

HOUSE ELEPHANT

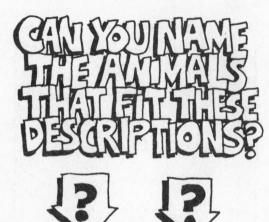

1. This animal has been bred in nontropical parts of the world for both its meat and its coat. The coat produces fibers which are used to make a long-lasting fabric. The animal is noted for its strong grouping instinct and grazes with others of its kind in large flocks.

2. Adapted for life in very dry areas, this animal can go for long periods of time with no food or water. Man has used it for milk, meat, and transportation.

3. This very large animal has been used to carry very heavy objects, such as logs. It is known for its giant size, long nose, and its pair of huge upper incisor teeth, which are highly prized by man.

4. This bird spends most of its time on the ground. The races of this species have been bred by man for meat or egg production.

5. This animal has a diet very much like that of man—it eats practically anything. It has been bred to be of large size, since man uses it as a source of meat. The legs are short and the body stocky.

6. Here is an animal noted for having a mind of its own. In spite of this reputation, this horned animal has been domesticated (tamed) in many parts of the world and is an important milk animal. Most varieties have beards.

The genus name is given for each animal. 1. *Ovis*, sheep, highly valued for its wool. 2. *Camelus*, camel, found in two species (one-hump and two-hump), very important in some desert regions of the world. 3. *Elephas*, Indian elephant, long domesticated in Asia, has ivory tusks. 4. *Gallus*, chicken, can fly, but most varieties are not very good at

it. 5. *Sus*, pig, one of the closest to man in terms of what it eats, an important food itself in some parts of the world. 6. *Capra*, goat, well adapted for the rugged life of a mountain animal, will try to eat practically anything.

CHAPTER FOUR
LEARNING THE ROPES

OKAY, SON...FIRST YOU GO TO THE DOOR AND MEOW...WHEN THEY OPEN THE DOOR, YOU STAND THERE LOOKING OUTSIDE FOR A LONG TIME... THEN YOU TURN AROUND AND GO BACK TO THE EASY CHAIR... ...GOT THAT?

Animal watching is a fascinating business. You can't help wondering sometimes what makes animals do the things they do. How do bees know where to find the nectar and pollen they need, and what makes salmon return to the same streams where they were hatched?

This kind of behavior is called *instinctive*—it does not have to be learned. Instinctive behavior is controlled by genes, as much a part of the animal package as, say, an anteater's long snout.

Humans have some instinctive patterns of behavior, too, but very few compared with other animals. You don't have to watch people very long to realize that most of what you see them do is a result of learning. How we learn to behave is the subject of what comes next.

Adapting to Everywhere

Animals have developed some remarkable adaptations in order to survive. In the colder places on Earth, fur, feathers, and fat help warm-blooded animals make it through harsh winter conditions.

That isn't the whole story. Those physical adaptations wouldn't be enough without adaptations in behavior as well. How could a grizzly bear survive without hibernating through the coldest months, or a robin live until spring unless it flew to places where snow doesn't cover the ground?

Humans are much the same. Our lack of protective covering alone would seem to be enough to keep us away from the colder parts of the world. But we have developed special patterns of behavior that let us live in areas where even our furry and feathered friends can't make it.

People don't rely on instinctive behavior patterns the way the hibernating bear and the migrating robin do— patterns that all members of their species know to follow without having to learn them.

Instead, humans have developed a very special way of doing things. This has made it possible for us to live not only in the freezing cold, but also in the heat of the tropics. This adaptation is called *culture*.

CULTURE

Culture is a way of life and the things which that way of life produces. It is based on learned behavior. Instead of being guided by biological messages, people do things as they do because they have *learned* to do them that way. Culture is learned by people and from people.

Think about your own behavior. Which of the following behaviors are guided by instinct, and which are learned cultural patterns?

1. Jumping when someone pops a balloon.

2. Deciding to eat a hamburger.

3. Making a tree fort out of lumber and plywood.

4. Getting into pajamas before going to bed.

5. Listening to a friend tell a joke.

Jumping when someone pops a balloon is a physical reaction to loud noise; it's more instinctive than cultural. The balloon itself is a part of your culture, something man-made.

Hunger is also a physical thing, but eating a hamburger is an action that has a cultural basis. What made you decide to eat it when you did? Why a burger instead of a handful of grasshoppers? This one is part instinct, but also a cultural type of behavior.

Your tree fort might be something like the nests chimps build by instinct —a place to feel protected and to rest

in. But by building it out of materials that had to be shaped for the purpose of building, you are carrying out a cultural activity. How did you know how to build it? You had to learn a lot of things about materials and tools to do that.

Sleeping is another biological, instinctive necessity. Putting on pajamas (a specialized type of clothing) before you go to bed each night, though, is cultural. Just ask that chimp without pajamas up there in the tree.

Listening to a friend tell a joke is a highly cultural activity. Other animals play and have jokes of their own, but man seems to be the only one who uses language to create pictures in the minds of his fellow creatures. So we're also the only animal who has to listen to bad jokes and suffer by knowing their meanings.

Sometimes it's difficult to draw an exact line between behavior that is based on your physical makeup and behavior based on culture. That's no accident, because you are a product of both your biological and cultural heritage.

Saying a Mouthful

Communication is very important in the animal kingdom. Dogs bark to let others know that they should keep their distance, birds give warning calls when danger approaches, and chimps greet each other with friendly grunts and hoots. These examples of vocal-auditory (sound) communication show that animals find it useful in their everyday lives.

No form of animal communication is as versatile as the sound communication of humans that we call language. Language is so important that without it we wouldn't have culture as we know it.

For now let's look at one of the practical uses of language. You'll need three willing friends, a watch or clock with a second hand, and something to hide. Candy would be a good choice because it gives your searchers a good reason to look harder, but anything will do.

The idea is for you to hide your object somewhere in a room, in a place that is out of sight. Each of your friends will get a chance to find it, but each will get different kinds of clues. The first searcher has the toughest job, so get a volunteer who thinks he or she is very good at finding things.

All you tell the first searcher is what the object is, and that it is somewhere in the room. Then start timing. Make sure that the other two don't get a chance to see inside the room until their turns.

When the first searcher has found the object and you have noted the time it took, put the object back in exactly the same place. The second searcher can get some help from the first, who is allowed to stand in the doorway and make any gestures or noises, *except* words of the human language. The second searcher can't talk to the first, either. Start timing when the second one enters the room, and stop as soon as the object is found.

The third searcher gets a different kind of help from number two. This time, the second searcher can stand in the doorway and talk to the third one. Hide the object again and start timing.

What did you find out about the usefulness of language in this situation? The gesture and noise communication gives a searcher an advantage over one who has no clues, but language gives the third searcher an even greater edge. How would a searcher have done if verbal directions had been given *before* he entered the room? It is the kind of clue that only language can give—a picture of how something not immediately present will be, before we actually are there to experience it.

Sounds Right

Take a variety of sounds, put them together to make words, combine the words into sentences, and you are building a language.

Of all the things you are likely to learn in your lifetime, language is probably the most difficult and the most useful. It's amazing how far you have already come—you didn't know any words when you were born. The dozens of different words you use every day in speaking with the people around you had to be learned, just as you had to learn how the sounds are put together to make words.

We humans have special physical equipment to help us make the variety of sounds we use in everyday speech. A few birds are able to imitate human speech, but even our closest relatives can't produce many of the sounds used in our languages.

How do we make all those different sounds? Very slight differences in the way our speech organs change or stop the flow of air coming out of our lungs

71

make the variety of sounds possible. We make very slight changes in our speech organs to produce that variety of sounds. The way our lips, tongue, vocal cords, and nasal passages move and the other ways we stop the flow of air from lungs to mouth account for these differences.

Sit or stand in front of a mirror and see how you make these little changes in forming words. Say the names "Nan" and "Dan." Can you hear a distinct difference between them? Look at

your lips and tongue. Are you moving them the same way when you say the two names? If you are, then what accounts for the difference? Try "man" and "ban" and see if that helps you find the difference.

You can't really *see* what that difference is, since it happens inside your mouth. But you can *feel* the difference if you close off your nose by pinching it between your fingers. Now say the words and listen for the differences between "Nan" and "Dan," "man" and "ban."

When you say "Nan" and "man," you keep your nasal passages open, and you close them off when you say "Dan" and "ban." That's why it becomes difficult to hear the differences when you close your nose with your fingers.

Next try these pairs of words: "Dan" and "tan," "van" and "fan." Are your lips and tongue in the same place for each pair? What's the difference here?

Put your fingers around your throat and feel what happens when you say each of the four words. What you are feeling is the vibration of your vocal cords when you say "Dan" and "van" (the *d* and *v* are *voiced*). The sounds of the *t* and *f* are *unvoiced,* which means there is no vibration when they are sounded.

Little differences like the ones you have just felt are used to make the sound units, or *phonemes,* of every language. Some English phonemes are lacking in other languages (notice that you don't find any *l*'s on Japanese maps—it's a sound the Japanese don't use), just as some of the phonemes of other languages are missing from English. The speakers of one language can be taught the phonemes used in any other.

Our ape cousins don't seem to be able to learn many phonemes. A few chimpanzees have been taught to speak a handful of words from human languages, but they are physically unable to get beyond this point. Human speech just isn't their strong point.

That doesn't mean that apes can't learn to use human language to communicate. A number of them have been trained to use human sign language, and taught a fairly large vocabulary.

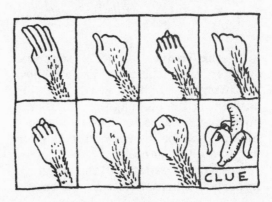

One ape that really knows how to use sign language is a gorilla named Koko. She has learned to use hundreds of different signs and even combines them into sentences. Koko and a few other apes have shown us that we can communicate with our closest relatives if we are patient and let our fingers do the talking.

You Don't Mean . . .

The words we use in language are not a useful means of communication unless there is a common understanding of what they mean between the speaker and listener.

"Yerkz Hedja Blimpet," says the speaker. If the listener doesn't know the meaning of those words and the patterns of the language, the message doesn't get across. The speaker's meaning can be interpreted in English as "I hate this game."

Why are the patterns of the language important to know? Because the speaker could have used the same words—in a different order—and the meaning would have been entirely different. "Hedja yerkz blimpet" means "This game hates me."

Trying to understand a different language, or having to learn a new one, gives you a real appreciation of how well you have learned your own, and how difficult it is to learn another.

But there is even more to learning language than this. In order to get their true meanings, you have to learn a lot about the way people say things, and watch the gestures they make while saying them.

Let's say that you go to a nursery (a place that takes care of children, or one where plants are grown?) with mom to buy a maple. Your mom wants

74

to know how much water to give the young tree and asks, "Should I water it a lot during the first year?" The nursery salesperson answers, "You can't water it too much."

Did the salesperson mean that she shouldn't give it very much water, or that she couldn't hurt it by giving it lots of water? Either answer could be right, depending on the tone of voice the salesperson used. And what is "too much" water?

How about the following situations?

Your friend Chris comes back from the zoo, where she went with her brother, even though she had wanted to go skating instead. She says, "We had a *great* time at the zoo!"

Uncle Roscoe is telling a story to your kid brother about the turtles he saw at the zoo. "They were so big," he says winking at you, "that I saw a whole herd of mountain goats climbing around on one of 'em."

"You're not gonna believe this," says Todd, "but a couple of ugly-looking purple creatures with six arms and gooey stuff all over them grabbed me and ate that piece of cake my mom sent over for you."

Answers: The speakers don't mean what they are saying—the first one means just the opposite, the second is stretching the truth, and the third is probably lying (unless the goo on Todd's face is *not* chocolate).

Normal

Most of us feel that we decide for our-selves how we should act and what we should do. At least, that's the way things are supposed to be with grown-ups—no one tells them what to do. But they also have rules of behavior that are just as important for them as the ones your parents set down for you.

Every culture has its own *norms,* or standards of "normal" behavior. Peo-ple can choose how to act and what to do, but their choices have to be within the limits defined by that culture.

Let's look at clothing, for example. Everyone can choose what to wear as long as it is within the limits consid-ered normal. What if someone wears

socks of two different colors to work? People might consider that to be odd behavior, and there might be a laugh or two among those who noticed. If that person didn't wear socks or shoes to work, there would be even more ridi-cule.

This kind of behavior is outside the *folkways* of our culture. Breaking with these customs is not considered very serious, but those who do break with them are often laughed at or have fun made of them. Most of us can't stand the embarrassment of being laughed at by others, so we try to go along with, or conform to, the folkways.

What if the oddball shows up at work wearing no clothing at all? Now we are

moving into behavior that violates the *mores* (sounds like what parents like to see on report cards—more *A*'s) of a culture—rules that are seen as necessary to the welfare of the society. The violator would be likely to lose the job, and some people would be shocked or angry. Most people feel such behavior is a "threat" to society, and that it can't be allowed to continue. Kids and some adults often have a different reaction to such "shocking" behavior. They sometimes find it very funny, but they still feel some of the shock.

Cultures that have developed writing set some of their mores down as *laws,* and set standard punishments for those who break them. In some cultures jail or taking away prized possessions is not used as punishment. Small communities sometimes punish "wrongdoers" by not speaking to them or by banishing them from the community entirely. If you think this isn't much punishment, just imagine everyone

you know turning their backs on you whenever they see you!

Here are some situations you might run into. Which ones are normal; which ones go against the folkways of your culture; which ones violate the mores; which of them are against the law?

1. One of your friends says that she doesn't like to play a game everyone else enjoys.

2. A boy in your class shows up at school wearing a dress.

3. Your kid brother goes out in freezing weather without his coat.

4. Someone at the movies breaks in line ahead of other people.

5. An uncle steals money from your grandfather.

6. You find your dad sitting alone, shouting at the TV.

Answers: 1. The friend that doesn't like the game is not following the norms of your group, but probably is within the folkways in not liking a particular game. Our own culture makes

allowances for differences of this kind, but kids in your group might make fun of her.

2. Wearing clothing considered "right" only for the opposite sex is usually considered a violation of mores, especially if it's done by males. The kid would probably get thrown out of school, and would be a target of lots of ridicule. Some entertainers make a living impersonating members of the opposite sex, however.

3. Your kid brother might be going against folkways (and your parents' rules for sure!) going out in the cold without a coat, but he probably would be considered normal—"just a kid." Age is taken into account when people judge behavior, and kids sometimes get a break.

4. Breaking into a line of people who are waiting lies somewhere between a violation of mores and a violation of folkways. The seriousness of the offense (and its punishment) depends on who does the breaking in. A very young or a very old person might not arouse as much anger as someone in between. This kind of behavior could lead to sharp words or even a fight.

5. The uncle could find himself in serious trouble. Most people would con-

sider this a threat to the general welfare, behavior that "cannot be tolerated." Since the stealing took place within a family, the punishment depends somewhat on the feelings of the individual family members. So this is an example of a situation where formal law might not be used, but the punishment of shame within the family is considered almost as severe as jail.

6. Your father's behavior could be considered very normal under the right circumstances. Can you guess what they would be? That's right—although it would be "abnormal" for anyone to yell at the TV in most situations, people who share our culture think it is normal for sports fans to cheer for their favorite teams, players, and horses.

Right and Wrong

Do you know right from wrong? What kind of question is that? It's a question of values.

Just as every human *society*—a group of people sharing a common culture—has rules of behavior, it also has a set of values which underlies the rules. The rules may be "Don't pick flowers out of Mrs. Weedley's garden," "Ask your sister before borrowing her pen," or "Never take anything from a store without paying for it," but the principal value underlying them is "You should respect the property of others."

Common values are what give members of a society similar ideas of right and wrong. Sometimes problems arise between members of different societies (who therefore have different cultures) as a result of these differing values.

For example, the way European settlers and many American Indian peoples looked at the ownership of land led to conflict. Europeans "claimed" what they saw as "unused" lands, defending

them with weapons when they felt threatened. The native inhabitants saw land as belonging to all the people, not to be claimed or used by people as private property.

The result of this kind of value conflict was that the members of each society saw the other as "bad" or "evil." Europeans were inclined to think of the Indians as people who had "no respect for property rights" and who "act like savages." They used the fact that native peoples had different standards of dress, behavior, and beliefs as a reason for treating them like nonhumans.

Judging the behavior of people who have different cultures as "wrong" or "immoral" because it doesn't fit our own cultural patterns is called *ethnocentrism*. When nothing is known of another culture's values, ethnocentric views can lead to misunderstanding and intolerance.

According to your cultural values, how would you judge the following situations?

1. Adults walk around with sticks of fire in their mouths.

A D U L T S

2. People ride in chariots that crash into one another, sometimes killing themselves.

3. Special ceremonies are held for young people with the idea of stirring up hatred for an opposing group and a desire to defeat it in physical combat.

4. Many people sit for hours staring into boxes of light.

5. People use machines that make them so cold that they sometimes have to put on extra clothing in the summer.

6. Children who are not allowed to use force with each other view fights and killings in their own homes.

7. A group of people is trained especially to kill others.

Do you feel that some of these actions are strange or weird, that they could only be part of a crazy culture? Consider that these are just unusual descriptions of things that are a part of everyday living in your own culture!

The terms we ordinarily use to describe the situations you have just read about are smoking, riding in cars, rallies that take place before sports events (such as school football games), watching TV, air conditioning, violence in TV shows (including cartoons), and the armed forces in peacetime as well as in war.

Others

Sometimes there are rivalries between groups within the same society. There may be an example of this rivalry in your own school—two groups of people who see each other as "bad." In this case there probably are not very many differences in values, but mostly in style.

Any differences that do exist between members of the two groups are made to seem much greater than they really are. The way people act, dress, and talk is seen by members of the other group as evidence that they are not as "good."

Even if you have been lucky enough not to have seen much of this kind of behavior (or been involved in it your-

the question or the answer. Write down the things they say. When you have several answers, find a group of people from your school and ask the question to the whole group. Try not to influence the answers; let your schoolmates answer for themselves.

Were there any differences between the things you heard from individuals and those you heard from the group?

If the things you heard from people in the group were worse, it has something to do with the "us and them" feelings that groups often promote. People in our society (and others too) often try to make themselves feel better by thinking that they are "better" than members of other groups.

self) within your school, you may have heard uncomplimentary things said about a rival school. Sports events sometimes bring out hostility toward people who attend the other school.

You can find out what types of things people at your school think about kids who go to a rival school (pretend its name is Ratsly) by asking a simple question: "What's different about the kids who go to Ratsly?"

First ask a number of people individually, where other people can't hear

The kind of people you chose to ask could account for a difference in the answers you got too. Maybe you happened to talk to a real Ratsly hater, or even a group of them. And what about the sex of the people you asked—were they boys or girls? What difference would that make?

If you are really dedicated, you should try going to good ol' Ratsly and asking the same question about *your* school. Remember that what you hear there might be affected by the fact that you are from the other school. Are there any similarities in the things they say about your school and the things you heard about theirs? Do you consider what you wrote to be true?

On Stage

Have you ever thought of yourself as an actor? No, not just because you were in a school play or played the part of a camel in a Christmas pageant once. As a member of society you are on stage every day.

Here's how the production works:

The parts you get to play in this show are called *roles*. Just as in the school play, you don't get to choose your own parts—your roles are determined by the other actors who are on stage with you.

The script that tells you and the other actors what to do is your culture. You get to choose some of your own lines and how you will deliver them, but you have to follow the outline of the script.

You and the other actors perform before an audience made up of the members of your society. If you play your roles well, you are rewarded with acceptance; but if you don't, the audience will show its disapproval.

All of this may seem farfetched, so let's look closer at how this works. Which of these parts have you been given to play in your everyday life: sister/brother, son/daughter, neighbor, student, friend, classmate, enemy, customer, passenger, stranger, big kid, reader?

Probably most of these (and perhaps all of them) are roles you play daily. Right now you are in the role of a reader, supposedly curious and interested in the things you see on these pages. As the writer of this book, my role is to make what you read enjoyable enough that you keep on reading.

A SATISFIED READER

Each role listed above has a counterpart role connected with it. There has to be a parent if someone takes the role of child, just as there can be no customer without someone to play the role of a salesperson. We get so used to dealing with other people in these counterpart roles that we could switch roles with them and do a pretty good job of playing their parts.

PARENT ROLE

CHILD ROLE

Perhaps you would like to find out how well you can play other people's roles: take the part of one of your parent's good friends. You are going to play this role in front of one or both parents, so make sure you can give a convincing performance.

This may not be as difficult as it sounds. You have often watched the person whose role you will play, which means you already know how this friend talks to your parent, the kind of language as well as the kinds of things

CINNAMON ROLL

talked about in conversation. You also know the way that person is likely to react to what your parent does and says.

Make yourself think the way you suppose your parent's friend thinks, and start the conversation the same way that person would. Stick with your part as long as you can.

How long did it take before your parent figured out whose part you were playing? To be convincing, you have to be able to understand your parent's role as well as the friend's.

What if you want an increase in your allowance? Put yourself in your parent's role for a moment to find out the reasons why you might not agree with the request. Now think of the arguments that might persuade you to go along with the extra money. If you can do this kind of role-playing well, you probably have a fairly easy time understanding why other people do the things they do, and maybe even getting them to see things your way too.

Act Your Age!

The roles you are expected to play change as you grow up. There was a time when your social position (or *status*) was that of "baby," with only baby roles to play. You weren't expected to wash dishes, tie your own shoe laces, or fix yourself a sandwich for lunch.

Those things are part of what you had to learn in taking on the roles of "big kid." Much of that learning took place while you watched others perform their roles. Older brothers or sisters, big kids in your neighborhood, and your parents all provided you with *role models* to imitate.

You may have gotten yourself into trouble imitating older people. Some of the things adults do are considered *too* adult for younger people, and, in fact, are forbidden. Parents sometimes go out of their way *not* to do some things around their children even though they would like to do them. It's because kids are good imitators.

...OH DEAR MOTHER AND FATHER, YOU HAVE BEEN SUCH WONDERFUL PARENTS ALL THESE YEARS. I AM THE LUCKIEST GIRL IN THE WORLD! YOU ARE SO KIND AND LOVING AND INTELLIGENT AND... AND... **GENEROUS!** THAT'S THE WORD I'M LOOKING FOR! I JUST KNOW YOU WANT ME TO HAVE 50¢ MORE A WEEK BECAUSE YOU LOVE ME SO VERY MUCH AND... ETC... ETC... ETC...

Imitating adult roles is not just fun and games for younger children. It's a way for them to try out roles that they will be expected to play in the future. All of us older people learned parts of our grownup roles while we pretended to be police officers, nurses, teachers, and cow punchers when we were kids.

AUTHENTIC
COW PUNCHER

One thing we aren't supposed to do is to take on the roles and behavior of younger people. Other actors on our stage—and sometimes even people in the audience—remind us, "Act your age!" They tell us that acting out younger roles is immature and irresponsible behavior.

Would you expect members of our society to judge the actions of the following people as too old, okay, or too young for their ages?

1. A two-year-old crying for his or her mother after being left at the babysitter's house.

2. A sixth grader with a teddy bear in a school desk.

3. An eight-year-old smoking a cigarette.

4. A twelve-year-old entering college.

5. A ninth grader learning to drive a car.

6. A grandmother watching Saturday morning cartoons.

7. A four-year-old watching the late-night movie.

8. A second grader crying for his or her mother at school.

Answers: 1 and 5 are probably okay—this behavior is considered normal for that age; 3, 4, and 7 are doing things most people would feel are too old for them; 2, 6, and 8 are doing things considered too young for their ages.

86

Boy/Girl/Boy/Girl

1. ( ) screamed and jumped on a chair when the mouse ran across the floor.

2. ( ) went hunting and fishing at every opportunity.

3. ( ) put the roast in the oven to help get an early start on dinner.

4. ( ) hit the ball so hard that it cleared the fence for a home run.

5. ( ) picked up a small child and stopped it from crying.

6. ( ) reached over and gave the other kid a smack on the back.

7. ( ) loved to go through the trunks of the grandparents' old clothing.

8. ( ) came back from the pond wet and muddy, pockets full of frogs.

If you had to complete these sentences by putting "she" or "he" in front of each one, which would you choose? Go on and try them all.

Chances are that you put "she" in front of the first one, "he" in front of the second one, and continued alternat-

ing them that way throughout the rest of the list. If so, why?

It isn't because boys can't do the things you put "she" in front of, any more than girls can't do the ones where you put a "he." What you are seeing here is how society influences our thinking about the roles and behavior expected of each sex.

Boys and girls start out very much the same in every society, but they are quite different by the time they are grownups. Some of this is due to the physical differences between men and women, but much more is because of the different roles society expects females and males to play.

Hey, you aren't one of those people who goes around with the idea that girls are weak and boys are strong, are you? Then you must not know about many cultures where women do most of the hard physical work.

The Status Game

"Good afternoon," says the store owner cheerfully. "May I help you find something? We just received a shipment of designer dresses this morning

that would look very smart on you. I'll be more than happy to show them to you if you like."

"Keep your eye on that woman over there," whispers the store owner to the clerk. "I don't know what she's doing in here dressed like that, but I think she's up to no good."

The place and the speaker in these two incidents are the same, but something is different about the two customers. What do you think that difference is?

You have probably seen situations like this, where people are treated differently according to how they look. This particular example has to do with the way the store owner sees the *status* of the two customers.

The thing to remember about status in the dress-shop story is that not all statuses are considered equal. Our culture rates some statuses as being better than others.

Most people in our society today live in cities where they don't know most of the people around them. The only way

WHICH OF THESE WOMEN WOULD GET THE BETTER TREATMENT AT A FINE RESTAURANT? AT A BANK? AT AN EXPENSIVE STORE?

THIS ONE?

YOU'RE PROBABLY RIGHT... BY THE WAY, THAT'S THE SAME WOMAN, ON YOUR LEFT, AT THREE O'CLOCK IN THE AFTERNOON.

they have of judging other people's status is by what they can see. So in our culture the visible signs of a person's status are what we use to estimate that person's status. The outward signs of this social rank are called *status symbols,* and some people go to great lengths to get and show off as many of these symbols as they can. They are playing the status game!

Actually there is more than one set of rules in this game. People with a lot of money sometimes are very careful to avoid showing off their wealth openly. They score higher in their game by *not* flashing status symbols when they have the chance.

1. Jeans that are very sturdy and will last a long time, made by a company known for making work pants.

2. Jeans that look like more expensive designer ones, but cost less and have a little-known label.

3. Jeans that are very expensive and have a famous designer label that everyone can see.

For people playing this kind of status game, two things are very important. The things they buy have to be expensive, and other people must be able to see that they are expensive. Does this help explain why labels are so important to the players?

Players who are not so rich have other rules. If you have ever heard people brag about how great their things are compared with someone else's you have seen the more ordinary version of the game. Which pair of jeans do you think the not-so-rich game-player would choose?

90

Clothing is often used as a status symbol, but there are others as well. Which kinds of cars are status symbols among the people you know? What about neighborhood—can you name a part of town near you that gives the people who live there higher ranking on the social scale than people who live in other parts of town? Does the sound system that one of your friends owns give him or her higher status in your group?

One way to see how status and its symbols can be different from one part of society to another is to think over your answers to these questions and compare them with the way your parents would answer them. Which cars impress your parents? Do you know any symbols of status that are important to them that don't seem important to you? Some of the rules of the game change as people get older too.

You may once have heard someone say, "Why does he insist on playing with that ragged doll instead of the new one we just paid so much for?" or "I wish she would wear that nice new blouse and throw away that nasty old T-shirt." Younger kids don't know how expensive things are, and they don't care anyway. As with other parts of culture, the status game and its rules have to be learned.

CHAPTER FIVE
DAY IN, DAY OUT

Culture gives us ways of dealing with everyday living. Take the problems of living in a cold climate, for example. You aren't born knowing how to keep warm in the harsh winter cold, but your culture has developed standard ways of dressing warmly, finding food, and heating your home. As you look around, you find many other people doing things the same way you do, and it's not a coincidence.

We get so used to doing (and seeing others doing) things a certain way that we find ourselves thinking that people everywhere share an instinctive "human nature." They don't. People who have other cultures do things differently, and they see *their* own ways as "human nature."

This chapter deals with some of the common problems of everyday living that all humans share, and the sometimes different cultural patterns of handling them.

You Are What You Eat

Do you ever wonder about the things that you see other people eat for lunch? How is it possible that some people love cream cheese and jelly sandwiches and other people can barely stand to look at them?

We all have our individual tastes for certain foods; some things we like to eat, others we hate. Many of our likes and dislikes have to do with our culture and how we have learned to look at what is and isn't "food."

Below on the right is a list of the things that you and your family might eat—things that our culture has defined as food. On the left side are descriptions based on the way a visitor with another cultural tradition might view them. Match the description with our culture's common name for the "food."

a. pig ears, snouts, tails	1. mushrooms
b. unformed chicken embryo	2. tripe
c. common fungus	3. drumstick
d. cattle rump muscle	4. cheese
e. thistle bud	5. bologna
f. hind leg of a hog	6. maple syrup
g. sour milk solids	7. artichoke
h. tree sap	8. roast
i. bird leg	9. egg
j. ox stomach	10. ham

MMM! A PIG EAR, SNOUTS, AND TAILS SANDWICH!

Answers: a-5, b-9, c-1, d-8, e-7, f-10, g-4, h-6, i-3, j-2. Which list sounds better to you?

Food for Thought

Most animals are specialists when it comes to food. Anteaters are very choosy about their chow, although they will eat termites just as eagerly as they will the ants from which they get both their name and much of their nutrition. Their bodies are so well adapted to this kind of diet that these insects are the only kind of food anteaters can eat.

Not many animals are as picky when it comes to eating as anteaters, but most tend to specialize in eating either plants or other animals. Plant eaters are called *herbivores* (URB-uh-vorz), and *carnivores* (KAR-nuh-vorz) are the animals that eat (no, not automobiles) meat.

Which of the animals listed below are carnivores and which are herbivores?

sheep	dogs
snakes	gorillas
kangaroos	horses
pandas	humans
cats	rabbits
bears	sharks

HUMAN TEETH ARE MULTIPURPOSE

Answers: Carnivores: snakes, cats, dogs, sharks; herbivores: sheep, kangaroos, pandas, gorillas, horses, rabbits. Two of the animals (bears and humans) are missing from both lists. That's because they are herbivorous and carnivorous—which makes them part of neither group. Bears and humans are part of a relatively small group of animals known as *omnivores,* who regularly dine on both plants and animals.

Humans are able to eat such a varied diet because we have a generalized digestive system and multipurpose teeth. We are able to get some nutritional value out of almost anything, although we are not as efficient at digesting vegetation as our ape cousins, or at handling meat the way our canine and feline (dog and cat) friends can.

If you take a close look at what people actually eat, you find that it isn't the same from one group to another. Culture gives us our idea of what is "food" and what isn't.

Some of these differences can be explained by the fact that the same plants and animals are not found in all parts of the world. Eskimo people living in the far north don't find bananas there; central African farmers cannot hunt seals to include in their diet.

There are many cases where an item that is considered "food" by people of one culture is not considered edible by people of another. Some Pacific islanders would be amazed to see you eat chicken eggs, since they don't consider them "fit to eat."

They would also be surprised to see you turn down a dish of turtle meat, a prized food in their culture. Both chicken eggs and turtle meat are nutritious things for humans to eat, but culture tells us whether or not they get the label of "food."

Here are some things that are considered food in other cultures, and are available to us. Which of them do we think of as food: dandelions, dogs, seaweed, garden snails, eels, acorns, bullfrogs, tomatoes?

Answers: Only one of these is widely defined as food in our culture. However, there are groups within our culture who eat each of them. Dandelions are eaten by some people as raw greens or as a cooked vegetable; or they can be used to make drinks, including tea and dandelion wine. Dogs are eaten in many parts of the world on occasion, although they don't make up

a big part of the menu anywhere. Seaweed is an important food among coastal peoples, supplying salt and trace minerals as well as vitamins. Garden snails, especially members of the genus *Helix,* are sometimes found in expensive French restaurants, called by the French name *escargot* (ess-car-GO). Eels are common on both sides of the Atlantic Ocean, but they are eaten much more frequently by Europeans than by North Americans. In some American Indian cultures acorns are carefully treated to remove the harsh tannic acid, then ground into meal and eaten. Frog legs are a gourmet treat sometimes found in the most expensive French restaurants.

What about the tomato? Yes, today it is eaten by nearly everyone, but less than a hundred years ago most people in our society considered it a poisonous weed! Cultural definitions sometimes do change.

How Long Until I'm Hungry?

One thing you would think is free from cultural influence is hunger. Regardless of *what* people eat, having a full or empty stomach is a physical fact.

What about right now. Do you feel hungry? Did you just look at a clock? Culture may not be able to change how full or empty your stomach is, but it has a lot to do with when and how often you feel hungry.

Babies have small capacities for food, and they have to eat often to keep from running out of fuel. Parents of young children often wake up tired in the morning because babies can't always make it through the night without having something to eat. Eating is just

about their most important biological requirement.

Older people don't have to eat so often to keep their bodies going. Even one large meal per day will do. Here's a chart that shows the hours of the day. At what times do you eat? If you eat more than once each day, which meal is the largest one?

Take a look at the time between meals. Do you wait the same amount of time after each one? How is it that you are able to go so long between your evening meal and the first meal the next morning? Why does the second meal come so close to the first? And why three meals?

People with other cultures find themselves getting hungry at different times than we do. Some find themselves eating a midnight meal before they sleep for the night. Others feel hungry only twice a day.

By knowing that you are a part of our society, an observer could predict that you will eat three meals per day (plus a

96

snack or two between them): at around 7:00 or 8:00 in the morning, near noon, and again at around 6:00 in the evening. The reason for this isn't that all humans get hungry at that time. It's because our culture gives us a tummy timetable.

Stalking the Wild Cheeseburger

Okamu spends most of the morning in her part of the sweet potato garden pulling weeds. They grow fast in the highlands of New Guinea where she lives, and girls like Okamu have to keep after them in order to insure a good harvest. She has brought with her some cooked sweet potato left over from last night's meal and a thick mixture of taro root sweetened with cane juice.

In the afternoon Okamu heads for one of her favorite spots on the lake. She likes to search the shallow waters for crayfish, a treat enjoyed by everyone in her family. But today the water is muddy and high from the recent rains, and she can't see the crayfish.

What Okamu does find at the lake are many insects trapped in the tall grass by rising water. She shakes bunches of grass so that the crickets, grasshoppers, and roaches hiding there fall into the water. Then Okamu picks them up and puts them in the hollow sections of bamboo that she carries in her belt.

The bamboo tubes are full of insects by the time she heads back to the sweet potato patch in the late afternoon. The ripe tubers she digs up there will add to the family's dinner. Those insects will be roasted in the fire for about half an hour, making a crunchy side dish to go with the main part of the meal.

Okamu knows all about how to find food in her native land, but the skills she has learned there wouldn't do her much good if she found herself in our

society. She would need an experienced guide to help her find food in the cities where most of us live.

Hey, you know your way around here — you could help her out. Just fill in the missing words (they are all part of your culture) needed to get her to the cheeseburger.

Okamu is hungry. She looks around the strange house for something to eat. Which of the rooms might contain food? Finally, she comes to one room, the _____(1), where she finds shelves filled with small cylinders. Most of them have funny pictures on them, and she even finds a few with pictures of babies. She wonders if that is what is inside, and turns away in disgust.

On the other side of the room, she finds a large metal box that makes a humming noise. She opens the ____(2), and finds that it is very cold inside. There are bottles there filled with a white liquid, ____(3), but nothing that she recognizes as food. In another part of the box, Okamu sees a ____(4) with its feathers removed, but she finds it is so hard she cannot bite into it — because it is ____(5).

Okamu decides that there is no food in this place, so she goes outside to look for something to eat. But instead of finding grass and trees, she sees more buildings and ____(6) speeding past her on hard paths of stone. She walks along the smaller path in front of the house in hopes of finding food.

Things are looking bad for her until she notices a smell in the air. The smell is like the roasting of the amburgu lizard her brother Jakebo once caught. She follows the smell until it brings her to a ____(7), where food is being prepared for people to eat.

She looks through the glass and sees that people are eating. This is the place! Okamu follows a group of people through the door, and heads for the slab of wood with the sign that says "Place your ____(8) here." A man on the other side of the slab asks her, "May I help you?" And she replies, "Amburgu."

The man asks her, "Do you want that with ____(9) melted on it, lady?" She nods. The only problem she still faces is that she doesn't know that she needs ____(10) to pay for the food. She thinks that it is much easier to find food in her own land, where all you have to do is grow it, raise it, or catch it.

ANSWERS

(1) Kitchen—the small cylinders she sees are canned foods, the others are jars of "baby food," not babies that are food; (2) refrigerator; (3) milk; (4) chicken, turkey, or duck—take your choice among the birds we commonly eat—and, of course, it is (5) frozen; (6) cars—or "traffic," as we call a lot of cars together; (7) restaurant; (8) order; (9) cheese—it's the thing we often melt on our amburgus; we generally buy the things we eat with (10) money.

What Shall I Wear Today?

It's a beautiful day today, warm and sunny. So you decide to go visit a friend. You walk over to your closet and take a look inside at your clothes. The clothing you choose to wear today will cover your (pick the answers from this list):

hair	abdomen
nose and mouth	hips and buttocks
neck and shoulders	thighs
arms	calves
wrists and hands	ankles
chest	feet

Did you decide to wear just enough clothing to cover your hair and ankles? Since the weather is so warm, why not? Does your choice of clothing have to do with other things besides the weather? Those other things are part of your culture.

We can be sure of this because we know that people with other cultures make different choices. A Tiwi boy from northern Australia would visit his friend with nothing on—boys and men in Tiwi society don't wear any clothes. A girl or woman of the Kapauku peoples living in western New Guinea wears only a bark wrap covering her hips, yet she wouldn't feel dressed most of the time without a long net covering her hair.

Although many peoples wear less clothing than we do, some would be shocked to see the parts of our bodies that we leave uncovered. Women in parts of North Africa and Southwest Asia would not be caught in public without veils covering their noses and mouths.

Even stranger to us is the cultural clothing prescription for women on the island of Yap in the western Pacific. They don't wear clothing to cover their breasts, but make certain that their thighs are always covered. Our bathing suits and shorts are shocking to them.

If all of this seems very strange to you, think about this: less than a hundred years ago, the mores of our culture (important rules) that had to do with clothing were very different than they are today. Back then neither men nor women could appear in public without a covering from neck to ankles. Even furniture had "skirts," so that people didn't have to look at their "limbs." Using the word "legs" was even considered a little shocking in polite company!

Ask a grandparent or some older person about how standards of clothing have changed since they were your age. In those days there were different answers to the question of "What shall I wear today?"

Gimme Shelter

If you've ever wanted to be an architect (someone who designs houses), here's your chance. Get a pencil and a piece of paper and draw a diagram of a house you would like to live in.

Start by drawing the outside shape of the house. Pretend that you are looking down on the house from above. Then fill in any details you like—rooms, furniture, whatever.

Once you have drawn your house and arranged it the way you want it—not before—take a look at the following guesses about the way it looks.

Chances are that the house you designed has four straight sides (rectangular) in its outside shape, or a combination of two rectangles; a number of separate rooms dividing the inside space according to the activities that take place there—this probably includes a living room, a kitchen, at least one bathroom, and bedrooms for the people living there; space enough for all the people in your family.

Hey, these guesses are easy. Anyone could have made them, since these things are all part of the shelters we call houses in our culture.

But if someone from another culture had designed a shelter, it might have looked very different. An Ngoni from southeast Africa, for instance, would not have made the outside shape a rectangle—it would have been a circle.

That isn't the only difference. Ngoni houses aren't divided into rooms the way your house is. There are spaces within the single room set aside for various purposes, but there are no walls to separate them. The Ngoni would have no kitchen, bathroom, or bedroom in a house design.

Many of the things you included inside your house are not found in the Ngoni model because the activities connected with them are done outside. By the standards of other peoples, such as the Ngoni, our houses are very large and self-contained. We sleep, prepare and eat food, clean ourselves, and even find entertainment inside our houses. The Ngoni do most of those activities elsewhere.

About the only general thing you can say about houses in all human societies is that they give people protection from the weather and a place to sleep. Our culture has made houses do much more than this.

ROUND CATTLE KRAAL

NGONI HOUSES

Getting the Point

One of the most interesting questions facing people who study man is this: When did the large-brained primate who walked around on its hind legs become a "human"? Most of these scientists agree that we became human when we developed the objects, ideas, and patterns of behavior that we call culture. The problem is figuring out when that took place.

As you can imagine, ideas and behavior are difficult to trace millions of years after they developed. The only cultural items we have been able to trace from the distant past are the objects we call tools. Where we find the earliest tools, we find the first evidence of creatures we can call human.

The earliest tools that have survived to the present (they are thought to be around 3½ million years old) may not seem very impressive to you. They appear to be little more than rocks with chips knocked off the sides. But those simple stone tools represent the earliest proof we have that man was changing things found in nature to suit his own needs. This use of tools to get things done is called *technology*.

One of the most useful items found in nature is a stick. Baboons and chimps use the sticks they find to help themselves get food. Various kinds of roots have always been an important food for humans, so it seems likely that sticks were also used by our ancestors.

Find a sturdy stick and try digging in the ground with it. Would your job be any easier if your stick had a sharper point? Can you find a sharp rock nearby to help you put a point on your stick?

Now take a big step forward. Find a way to get a sharper edge on your rock. You could drop a heavy rock on top of another one and hope to get a sharp edge when the rock cracks and chips. Can you do this? (*Caution:* watch out for two things. Don't smash your fingers and be extra careful not to get rock chips in your eyes.)

What kind of edge did you get? With this kind of a "pebble tool" you should be able to sharpen your digging stick. A sharpened point must have been very helpful to ancient peoples hunting for animals. Also, they found ways of attaching stone points to their sticks.

With simple tools like the ones described here, man began the development of material culture. Tools were giant steps forward. Little by little, they have led to the complicated machines and other tools you see around you every day, if you get the point.

Would You Dig a Drink?

Rakondu is very thirsty from the dust and hot sun of the dry season. He decides to visit the waterhole for a drink. Along the way he stops to pick a long dried reed from a nearby clump.

This waterhole was dug by Rakondu's uncle a few weeks earlier with the help of his stone ax, and is covered with a large rock that keeps burrowing animals out and moisture in. Rakondu pushes the heavy stone away, digging away the top layer of sand beneath.

Then he pushes the reed deep into the hole and sucks on it. This draws slightly gritty water into his mouth, which he quickly spits out. Rakondu sucks again, this time getting a mouthful of cool water to quench his thirst.

How do *you* go about getting a drink of water when you are thirsty? The difference between your way of doing it and Rakondu's points up differences in the technology of two cultures. Both cultures have devised ways of making sure that people get water, but the materials used by each are very different.

Most of the people living in our society would say that our way of getting water is simpler. All you have to do is to hold a glass under the spigot and turn the handle of the faucet. But that glass of water didn't get there without the help of a great number of tools and techniques. What work had to be done before you could turn on the tap and get your water? Can you trace the flow of the water and the tools that were used to get it to you?

At the very least, your water went through a system that involves (1) the collection and storage of water in a reservoir, or underground in a well; (2) the delivery of water through a system of underground pipes to your

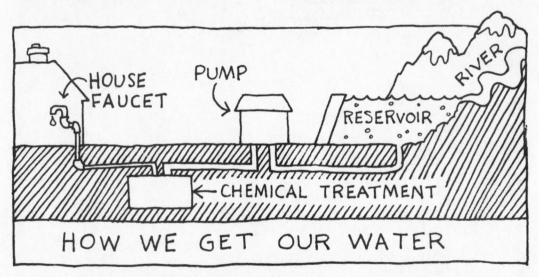

HOUSE FAUCET   PUMP   RESERVOIR   RIVER

← CHEMICAL TREATMENT

HOW WE GET OUR WATER

house; and (3) the plumbing inside your house that gets the water to the tap and controls the flow so that you get water only when you want it.

Along the way the water will probably have to be pumped, which is the case when it doesn't flow downhill all the way (it rarely does in cities). The pumps require lots of electricity. You could write many books just about the things we use and need to generate electricity. The water will probably be treated with chemicals, too, in order to assure that it is clean and healthy to drink when you get it in your glass.

The glass? Making the glass is another story in itself, a very complex process, like so many others needed to make the common objects we use every day in our society.

So maybe our way of getting a drink of water isn't so simple after all. The tools and techniques that Rakondu and his people use to get a drink are fewer and simpler in terms of the technology involved, even though actually getting a drink may take more effort on his part.

The important thing to remember about differences in the technology of various cultures is not that some are simple and others complex, but that both get the job done for the people who have developed them.

WHEW! THIS DIGGING FOR WATER IS MAKING ME THIRSTY!

CHAPTER SIX
A LOOK IN THE MIRROR

You probably consider yourself to be an individual who thinks and acts differently from anyone else in the world. To a visitor from Japan, however, your behavior may seem so similar to that of other people in the United States that you are a "typical American" to her. She notices that the way you dress, walk, greet other people, and even the way you carry your books, is very different from the way people do those things in Japan, but much like the way she sees other Americans doing them.

If you were to visit Japan, your reactions to the people there would probably be similar to their reactions to you; Japanese culture also has shared patterns of thinking and acting that an outsider soon notices.

Looking at cultures from outside can be something like looking in a mirror—the reflection you see there gives you a clearer picture of how you appear to others. More important, seeing your own culture through the eyes of another gives you clues to why you think and act the way you do.

Around in Cycles

One thing that is the same in every culture is the life cycle. People are born, live their lives, and die. But events like birth and death are more than the beginning and end of a person's life; they are passages between stages of the life cycle. Events of this kind are so important in most cultures that there are rites, or ceremonies, to mark them.

The first big event in the life cycle everywhere is birth. It's a time when people are very concerned about both mother and child, so a successful passage is cause for celebration. Among the Tiwi of Australia, the mother and newborn stay apart from other people for a week or two until it is considered safe for them to join other people. Then there is a ceremony at which the child is introduced to society and given a name of its own by the father. It has successfully made the passage from being an unborn human-in-the-making to becoming a new member of Tiwi society.

Can you think of any rites connected with birth that are a part of our culture?

Answer: Some proud fathers hand out cigars when they have a newborn child, and parents often mail cards (called birth announcements) to friends and relatives. Gift-giving that takes place at a baby shower is another kind of cultural recognition that society is receiving a new member.

Although children in our culture usually get their names at birth, there is a special naming ceremony known as "christening" or "baptism," at which time the name is formally recognized.

Going to school for the first time marks the passage when a child in our culture no longer spends most of the day at home with its mother or another adult. This first big step toward the world beyond home-sweet-home is like a change that takes place among Ngoni children, who live in southeast Africa. When an Ngoni child gets its first per-

manent teeth, it leaves home and begins sleeping in the house of a close relative. The Ngoni use a biological event instead of the calendar to mark this passage.

Puberty is a physical change that is recognized by most peoples of the world as the end of childhood and the beginning of adult life. For girls it is marked by the beginning of menstruation and changes in body shape (broadening of the hips and the growth of breasts).

Boys begin to change shape, too, with most of the broadening taking place in the shoulders and chest. Their voices change to a lower pitch, due to growth

in the size of the vocal cords and larynx. Both sexes show a change of hair growth patterns, with longer and coarser hair growing in the pubic area and armpits.

These physical changes that we call puberty don't happen all at once. They take place over a period of several years, usually starting at about age 12 or 13. They mark the beginnings of sexual maturity, the process that enables humans to reproduce. So puberty is an important passage in the life of every individual and the society.

Here's an account of the puberty rites among a group of people known as the Keeyan. They live in North America in the area between the Atlantic and Pacific oceans, bounded on the south by the Gulf of Mexico and on the north by the Great Lakes.

This account was recorded by the famous professor Ida Scribem of Tanzania, who now teaches at the Department of Anthropology (the scientific study of man), Great Rift University of East Africa. She spent many years living and working among the Keeyan, and has come to understand parts of their culture that we might find very strange or even comical.

Dr. Scribem writes: "I shall now describe that part of the Keeyan life cycle they call the 'looking-glass-time.' Unlike many other cultures, the Keeyan does not have a special ritual or ceremony to mark the passing from childhood to adulthood. Instead, the Keeyan youth struggles along during the years of the looking-glass-time, caught between the world of children and the world of adults, with one foot in each.

"I must point out that until the onset of puberty young people of both sexes show little concern for their own appearance. Most of them have to be forced to bathe regularly, and so they are usually grimy from head to foot. Such clothing as they wear is often ragged, dirty, and smelly, sometimes

PUBERTY CAN BE CONFUSING...

prompting parents to secretly throw it away or burn it.

"Keeyan children also take no special notice of the opposite sex at this stage, often forming mixed play groups. They view affectionate embraces between people of the opposite sex as disgusting, but they rarely are shy or embarrassed around children of the other sex.

"As Keeyan youngsters enter the looking-glass-time, there is a dramatic change. They are taught that dealings with members of the opposite sex are very dangerous at this time unless they shield themselves. This shield takes the form of the 'looking-glass-self,' which Keeyan youth use to hide the real self.

"The Keeyan consider the most important part of the shield to be the area of the head and face. Both sexes spend much time and effort with rituals involving the hair of the head. This they stroke with wands made of boar bris-

tles (or a boar-bristle substitute) and arrange with sharp pointed 'tooth-sticks.' Tooth-stick magic is so important to Keeyan youth that they carry tooth-sticks with them at all times.

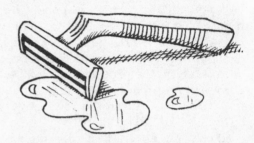

"The removal of some facial hair is another requirement of maintaining the looking-glass-self. Boys' rituals center around the newly growing chin and cheek hair, which may be nearly invisible to all but the individual himself. This is removed by scraping the skin with a sharpened flat piece of metal—an act that causes much pain and bleeding.

"The girls' rituals involve removal of stray hairs, especially around the eyes. These are pulled out one-by-one with a pinching tool made especially for this painful task. Girls use skin-scrapers, similar to the ones used by the boys, to remove hair from their legs and armpits.

"That is not the only torture to which Keeyan girls subject themselves in the rituals. Charms are often worn around the neck and wrists and on the fingers,

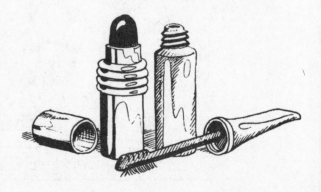

but earlobe charms are believed to contain even greater powers. Steel needles are thrust through the ears, and metal pins are stuck into the holes they make. After the wounds heal, charms are hung from the holes. Girls also coat their faces with paint and grease to hide the self beneath from danger.

"Besides changed attitudes toward members of the opposite sex, Keeyan young people treat members of their families differently during the looking-glass-time. They pretend younger brothers and sisters do not exist and avoid the company of their parents. This is partly due to the fact that parents often express disapproval of the youths' behavior. This behavior includes gathering in groups and staying up into the 'forbidden hours' listening to loud song-stories; lighting and sucking on the Keeyan sacred fire-weed sticks, which are reserved for their elders; wearing tight-fitting clothing,

part of the youths' looking-glass-shield and not traditional Keeyan attire.

"In order to understand the behavior of Keeyans during puberty, it is necessary to study their culture as a whole. Although much of this behavior seems absurd and makes little sense to outsiders, members of Keeyan society accept it as part of growing up."

Last Rites

We ordinarily think of death as the end of the life cycle. Death certainly is the event that marks the end of every person's life, but most cultures treat it as a beginning too. Dying is viewed as another passage from one stage of the life cycle to another. Ceremonies we call "last rites" usher people from the status of living members of society to the status of the dead.

The dead are treated in different ways by different cultures. In some, the dead are considered to be dangerous to the living, and their names are never even mentioned again. The Tiwi of Australia carry this a step further and change the names given to people by someone who has died, even if they were given the names thirty years before! Athabascan Indians of North America have so much fear of the dead

TYPICAL YOUNG KEEYANS

109

that they move away from places where people have died as quickly as they can, and don't return for many years.

Other cultures consider dead members helpful spirits who should be remembered often. There are some cultures, especially in southeastern Asia, where the bones or ashes of dead ancestors are kept in places of honor inside the homes of the living.

With attitudes toward the dead in various cultures being so different, it figures that last rites are not the same everywhere. Some cultures give the dead a big sendoff, complete with many "grave goods," or things that they may need in the afterlife stage of the life cycle. These can include tools, jewelry, food, clothing, and other valuable possessions. Other cultures simply bury the dead, or cremate them (burn them at very hot temperatures so that there is nothing left but ash), without preparing special tombs or grave goods for them.

Answer the questions below to see how much you know about how the American culture deals with death and the rites that go along with that passage.

1. What is the ceremony that is most often performed for a dead person?

2. How do we dispose of dead human bodies?

3. Do we have grave goods for our dead?

4. What special names do we use for people whose relatives have died?

Answers: 1. A "funeral" is what we call our last rites. 2. Our culture offers several ways of dealing with dead human bodies. The most common one is burial, where the body is placed into a coffin, or casket, then put into a deep hole in the ground called a "grave." A variation is to put the body into an above-ground tomb, crypt, or vault. In any case the body is kept in a special place—a cemetery—away from the living. Some people in our culture have their bodies cremated, and occasionally people who die at sea are wrapped up and slid overboard into the ocean (referred to as "Davy Jones's locker"). 3. Like many other peoples, Americans often send off the dead with some of the things they loved in life. This custom shows that we also consider death to be a passage rather than an end. People are frequently buried in their best clothes, and jewelry is sometimes left on the body. Caskets are very much like beds, and they look as though they are designed for comfort. 4. A person who was married to someone who has died is called a "widow" if the living one is a woman, a "widower" if the survivor is a man. People whose parents have both "passed away" are called "orphans" when they are not yet adults.

The Familiar

The family unit is very important in every human society. After all, our families are the people with whom we live; and we usually eat and sleep and share emotions, ideas, and experiences with them as well. Our family members are the people with whom we are most "familiar."

Your family also gives you your identity within society. Your family membership determines how others in society act toward you and respond to you while you are growing up. Even your name comes from this family identity—you are a "Miller," a "Johnson," a "Zilensky," or whoever—according to your family membership.

Who are the people living in your household, and what is their relationship to you? Chances are that they are all members of your *nuclear family*. That's the group (in any society) made up of the mother and father plus all of their children.

Today we are so used to this type of household arrangement that when we talk about our family we mean our nuclear family. But that isn't the whole story.

Monkey's Uncle

Take a look at this diagram. If you are A, and your mother is B, your father C, and your sister and brother D (that takes care of your nuclear family), who is E? And what about F and G?

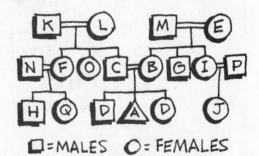

☐ = MALES ◯ = FEMALES

Answers: E is your grandmother, in this case your *maternal* grandmother, since she is your mother's mother (the Latin word for mother is *mater*). F is a person you would consider your *paternal* aunt; she is a sister to your father (*pater* in Latin).

What about G? That is your maternal uncle, and whether or not he considers himself to be a monkey's uncle depends on how he feels about you!

These relatives are all part of your *extended family*.

Kinfolks

Extended families are not important just because they make nice groups at Thanksgiving, or to give us convenient people to visit for weekends once in a while. They are the basis for the *kinship* system of every culture.

Who are your kinfolks? That depends on your culture. Take a look at that last diagram again. In some cultures you (A) would not belong to the same kinship group as C—your father! Even though you recognize the relationship of father and child, you would belong to the kinship group of B, your mother.

The kinship rules in a society of this kind are called *matrilineal,* since your kinfolk are the people on your mother's side of the family. F would not be your aunt in a matrilineal society the same way I would because I is a member of your mother's *lineage.*

Other cultures have *patrilineal* kinship systems. To determine last names, our culture generally follows this pattern: the members of your own family who have the same last name as you (or had the same last name before they got married) are members of your father's lineage.

If the kinship rules of a culture are patrilineal, which of the people in the diagram are in A's lineage? Which people are in the same patrilineage with B? Which share a patrilineage with J?

Answers: A's patrilineage includes the two Ds (the brother and sister), C (father), F and O (A's aunts), and K (grandfather). N and L are not members of the patrilineage, but are related only by marriage, and H and Q belong to N's patrilineage.

B shares a patrilineage with her brother and sister (G and I) and her father (M). The only person who is in the same patrilineage as J on the chart is P, her father.

What if the culture has matrilineal rules? Who shares A's matrilineage then? What's the relationship between A and J? Who shares H's matrilineage?

Answers: A's matrilineage on the chart is made up of A's sister and brother (the Ds), B and her sister I and brother G, E (A's grandmother), and J. Who is J in relation to A? They are cousins, first cousins according to our own kinship terms.

H shares his matrilineage with his sister Q, his mother F, and her sister and brother O and C, and his grandmother L.

Our culture has a kinship system that is *bilateral*—descent kinship is traced through both matrilineage and patrilineage. You are equally a member of your mother's and your father's families in tracing those kinfolks.

You may find it difficult to understand why extended families and kinship are such a big deal. In our culture today extended families don't have as much importance as they do in many other cultures, or as they once did in ours. That's because our culture has developed ways of providing many of the things we need in everyday living outside of our extended families.

If you could go back in time only a couple of generations, you would find that your extended family provided you with your way of making a living, place to live, education, recreation, and took care of you when you were sick or too old to work. Kinfolks still do these things for each other in many of the world's cultures.

Getting Hitched

A group of people from different cultures is watching a movie made in the United States of America. It's a movie where two young people meet at a dance, fall in love, and get married. They move away to another city and have children. Later on in the movie, the two quarrel with each other a lot, decide to get divorced, and go their separate ways.

When the lights come on, the viewers talk about what they have just seen on the screen. Most of them agree that the marriage was bound to fail, but they have different reasons for their conclusions.

One group comes from eastern Asia. They agree that the marriage had little chance of success because the choice of marriage partners was left up to the young people themselves, instead of elders in their families. "Surely these young people should not have been left to make such an important decision for themselves," says one. "The elders would have made a better match for them, and the bonds between the two families would have been stronger."

"It is easy to see why such a marriage might not last," says one East African viewer to another. "There was no bride price paid when the marriage took place. The couple could not have been serious about the arrangement, since no cattle were given to the bride's family to make up for their loss. They had no cattle to return when the marriage didn't work."

A group of American Indians from the Southwest feels that the young couple's decision to move away from their families to another city was to blame for the breakup of the marriage. "They should have moved in with the people of the wife's mother, of course," one says. "That way, the wife would have been able to ask her aunts and uncles to help with any disputes, and the husband could have gotten help from his mother's people too."

"It is quite easy to see the trouble in this situation," a Melanesian islander (from the southwestern Pacific Ocean) says. "The man needed another wife in order to improve the social position of his family. Without another wife and the children she would bring, he could not hope to increase his herd of pigs and bring honor to his father's people. His wife seemed opposed to the idea of taking another wife into her house, although this new wife would have helped her greatly with her work and brought her greater prestige."

What do you think of these explanations? They may seem very strange and mistaken to you; however, these people are simply judging what they saw on the screen by the standards of marriage in their own cultures.

That's a point you should remember when you hear about marriages arranged by elders, payments of "bride price," rules that specify where a newly married couple should live, and multiple husbands and wives in other cultures. Judging these things according to the marriage rules and practices of your culture makes no more sense than their explanations of ours.

One thing you can see from these stories is that marriage in other societies is more than an agreement between two people. It is a contract, or agreement, between their families as well. Marriage is a kind of "social cement" that holds together the whole kinship system in most cultures.

Do you see any traces of a contract between the two families in our own traditional wedding ceremonies? What are they?

Answers: There is a link with family arrangement of marriage partners in our custom of "giving away the bride," usually done by the bride's father or some other older member of her family. Some of the wedding gifts a newly married couple gets today are a type of property exchange between two families. In earlier times a bride gave a "dowry" to the groom. The dowry was property she got from her family, and in many ways appears to be the opposite of "bride price" paid by the groom's family in other cultures. In cases where a marriage didn't work out as expected, dowry or bride price might have to be returned.

Making a Living

Members of every animal species have to be able to eat, find safe places to live, and reproduce if the species is going to survive. Humans rely on culture to answer many questions about what work must be done to meet those needs, who will do the work, and how the products of the work will be shared among members of society.

Other animals don't have to be con-

115

cerned with who will do the work; each individual or small group provides its own necessities. Human societies, on the other hand, have some form of division of labor—work is divided up among people so that they don't all do the same things.

In cultures with relatively simple technology, the division of labor is usually based on sex and age. You'll find "women's work," "men's work," and particular work for children, older people, and middle-aged adults.

As some cultures developed their tool-using abilities more, there was sometimes a surplus of food, and people had time to spend doing other things. More necessities could be produced than people needed in order to live. In many cases the populations of these groups increased, but there was still more than enough to go around.

It was when there was more than enough to go around that people began to develop themselves as specialists, making a living doing work that is not part of the basic requirements of living. No longer was it necessary for every household to make its own cooking pots, for example, because someone might specialize in making them. In turn, that person could exchange pots for food and other necessities.

Division of labor in these kinds of cultures brought about great changes in the story of human life on Earth. Abundant food made it possible for people to live together in greater numbers (cities), and specialists began recording information in a special language (writing) that could last beyond the living memory of the oldest members of society. Most important, people in such cultures came to rely on each other to produce what they needed.

Our culture has carried this kind of division of labor to the point where most of us have very little idea of the work that others do.

One place where you do have a good idea of who does what is at your own house. Do you have a division of labor there? Which jobs are the responsibility of one person (at least most of the time), and which are shared?

washing clothes
taking out trash
watering houseplants
vacuuming floors
fixing breakfast
picking up mail
paying bills
grocery shopping
ironing clothes
changing lightbulbs
washing dishes
clearing the table

Supernatural

Humans may be the most intelligent animals in the world, but many of the things that happen around us seem to be outside of our control. There may be volcanoes threatening to erupt or serious illness spreading through the community. Plants and animals that supply food may be scarce; there may be too much rainfall, or not enough. People in all cultures are faced with problems such as these.

It hasn't rained for several weeks in Seco County, and the crops are suffering from a lack of water. Everyone is worried about the drought. Here are two things that are happening:

1. At Horace Freely's farm, a woman is placing willow sticks in lines along the ground next to Horace's dried-up cornfield.

2. Over at the Poplar Grove Church, a man is speaking in front of a crowd of people who have their heads bowed and their eyes closed.

Just what are these people doing? They are trying to do something about the lack of rain. These are examples of the kinds of things people in our culture might do when things are not going right.

117

At Horace Freely's farm, the woman —a rainmaker—is practicing the kind of behavior we often call *magic*. She is using the willow sticks in an attempt to control the forces of nature, or at least influence them enough to make rain fall. The idea behind this kind of magic is that the rainmaker must place the sticks (made of just the right material, willow) in exactly the right direction to get the results she wants.

The people at the church are taking part in behavior we call *religion*. The speaker, Reverend Paul Zinsky, is asking for help from a *supernatural* power. The people believe that this supernatural (above natural) force can control the forces of nature and make rain fall. According to the principles of religion, all of the forces of nature are under the influence of supernatural power.

There are many different kinds of religious ideas about the supernatural, just as there are many different cultures. People may believe that the supernatural lives in rocks and trees or is everywhere, that there is one supernatural force or many forces. Some religious beliefs say that supernatural beings have human form, while others insist that they look like animals, or have no shape at all.

TIKIS (MAN-GODS) ON EASTER ISLAND

In their dealings with the supernatural, religious people accept the possibility that the supernatural power may not answer their requests, or prayers, for help; people who practice magic think that by performing a ritual in exactly the right way, they will get the results they want. Magic may sound a little like *science* to you in this sense. Scientists repeat their experiments the same way again and again trying to find out how the natural—not supernatural—forces work.

Another way to look at the differences among magic, science, and religion is to see what happens if the things people do don't get the desired results. A magician would be likely to say that the ritual wasn't exactly correct or that some countermagic or stronger force was acting at the same time. A scientist would be likely to say that the scientific laws and principles used in the situation haven't been completely understood; something is missing. A religious person might say that the supernatural power didn't wish the results prayed for to happen.

Would you consider these goings-on in Seco County to be examples of magic, science, or religion?

1. Granny Gertson washes her car in the belief that it will rain afterwards.

2. Crash Gordon loads silver iodide crystals into his crop-dusting airplane so that he can "seed" the clouds when he thinks the weather conditions are right.

3. Joe Crofoot sings his medicine songs to Coyote, the water spirit, and asks for rain.

4. Johnny Kidder waves his hand, and water from a hidden garden hose wets a surprised group of onlookers.

You can see from some of these examples how magic, science, and religion sometimes are combined in the things people do. Granny's car-washing act is the kind of magic you often hear called "superstition" because scientific testing doesn't show a connection between clean cars and rainfall.

Crash's cloud-seeding is based on science; the crystals make it easier for moisture to collect in large enough particles so it is more likely to rain. Not very long ago, though, the idea of sprinkling crystals in the air to make rain would definitely have been considered magic.

The ritual songs that Joe sings are mostly religious, since he is asking Coyote (the supernatural) for help. Is Johnny a magician? His trick is something that we might think of as part of a magic show, but it is really based on the scientific principles that come into play when a hidden friend turns on the spigot and water shoots out of the hose.

Shalls and Shall-nots

Religion does other things besides keeping people from feeling helpless in times of trouble. The religious beliefs of every culture are an important part of the value system that gives people their sense of right and wrong. Religions teach that certain behavior is right because supernatural forces say it is correct to act that way; other behavior is wrong because it offends the supernatural. Which of these things are right or wrong behavior according to religions you know about?

1. Cutting trees in certain parts of the forest.
2. Wearing clothes in public.
3. Fighting with parents.
4. Eating the meat of animals.
5. Taking things that belong to other people.
6. Giving food to hungry people.
7. Living in a round house.
8. Catching fish if you are a woman.
9. Joking with your sister if you are a man.

Some of these things may strike you as strange subjects for shalls or shall-nots, but they are all examples of behavior that is considered right or wrong in the system of beliefs of some culture.

A Trobriand Islander would be just as surprised that your religion says that you shall wear clothing in public as you are to find that his religion tells him he shall not joke with his sister. In both cases the rightness or wrongness of behavior is based on the belief that the supernatural wants things to be that way.

Although many of the things we eat or don't eat have to do with personal taste and cultural tastes, there are also religious beliefs about which foods should and should not be eaten. There are even certain times when particular foods are forbidden, or *taboo* (a word from the Pacific islanders.)

Our own culture is different from most others in having within it many religions with somewhat different beliefs. Some of these religions have food and drink taboos, while others don't.

Here are things that are forbidden by one or more religions. Do you know which of our culture's religions consider them taboo?

meat of any kind
tobacco
alcoholic beverages
coffee and other stimulant drinks
pork
cough syrup

MY RELIGION FORBIDS DRINKING AND SMOKING.

MY RELIGION FORBIDS THE USE OF MODERN MACHINES.

PERSONALLY, I DON'T BELIEVE IN EATING MEAT...

How Things Came to Be

We humans are probably the world's most curious animal. When we are young and just learning about our culture and the world in which we live, we ask a lot of questions about how things came to be the way they are. All cultures are faced with these difficult questions, and cultures everywhere provide explanations called *myths,* which explain how the world was made, where people came from, and other mysteries from the very distant human past.

When you hear some of these myths, you may think of them as just old stories dreamed up by people with nothing better to do. If you look at them more closely, however, you'll find that they tell you many things about the living cultures of which they are a part. We are sometimes so interested in the storytelling part of a myth that we overlook what the myth says about the world and the people who live in it.

For example, the Hawaiian creation myth tells how Heavenly Father Tane gave his three sons responsibility for taking care of the world he had just created. The duties he gave to each one tell something about the way Hawaiians look at the world they see around them as well as introducing three important god-princes.

Myths used to be passed on by word of mouth from one generation to the next (they still are, in cultures that don't have written languages). After the invention of writing, myths could be recorded in print. Some of the myths handed down in our culture can be found in a book we know as the Bible.

If you take a look at the first part of the Bible, in the section called Genesis (which means "the beginning"), you will read about how the earth and man were created. You can also find answers to the following questions:

1. How was woman created?

2. What happened to the first human children?

3. Why did people begin wearing clothes?

4. Where did different languages come from?

Some people think that the Bible's explanations are a valuable part of our culture, but consider them to be just stories, not facts. Others feel that the writings found in the Bible are not myths; they believe that the accounts there are true and that things really happened just the way they are told.

Of course, peoples in other cultures have different accounts of creation. The Hawaiian creation myth says that the world came into being when a great white bird dropped an egg in the ocean, while the Cheyenne Indians believe that the world has always been here.

Myths also often give an explanation of why certain things are right or wrong; in other words, they help explain values. Some of the most basic values of our culture are found in the "Ten Commandments." According to the Bible, God gave them, written in stone, to Moses.

Other values can be found in myths other than those in the Bible. Some of these, like Bible stories, are based on historical events and people who actually lived. Do you know any stories about famous Americans that teach the value of always telling the truth?

Answer: Several stories tell about America's two best-known presidents, George Washington and Abraham Lincoln. Remember the kid who chopped down the cherry tree and then couldn't

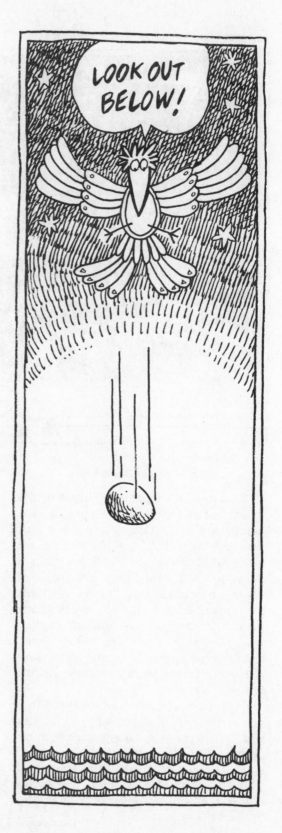

lie about it to his father? That was ol' George, our first president. The other president celebrated for his truthfulness is "Honest Abe" Lincoln.

HISTORY OR MYTH?

Other American heroes are recognized as being mythological for their courage (Daniel Boone, who wrestled a bear, and Davy Crockett, who died at the Alamo), inventiveness (Thomas Edison, the Wright brothers), and other traits that Americans value. The stories in some cases have outgrown the facts, but mythical heroes show great examples of the kind of behavior valued by their culture.

Yesterday, Today, and Tomorrow

If dinosaurs had developed culture, they might still be around today. Instead, they developed into highly spe-cialized animals who kept the same patterns of behavior through millions of years. Conditions changed, but the dinosaurs didn't—no more dinosaurs!

Culture is a never-ending adaptation. It can change to meet new conditions, and it has allowed man to adapt to an amazing variety of situations.

All this change doesn't come about easily. Like living beings—human animals are an example—cultures are made up of many parts that fit together. In order to work smoothly, the parts have to work together without getting in each other's way. Changes that take place in any single part affect every other part in some way, just as they do in your own body.

We have a good example of how rapid change can create problems right here in our own culture. If you could go back in time to about the year 1800, you would find your surroundings very different from what they are today. Perhaps the greatest differences you would notice would be in the technology, the tools and material things of everyday living.

Imagine that you and your family are going to visit relatives living ten miles from your house. How would you get there and how long would it take? What things would you be doing on your visit?

In 1800 there were no cars, motorbuses, or trains. There weren't even any steamboats. The fastest way you could get to your relatives' house would be by horse-drawn wagon or coach. If the roads were good (and this would be unlikely, since most roads of that day were dirt), the trip would take you half a day.

Since the trip would take so long, you would have to stay overnight with your relatives. You might sit up with your numerous cousins—people usually had much larger families in those days—but not watching TV or playing video games, since it would be another 150 years before TV would be invented. You and your relatives would have to make your own entertainment, which could include telling stories or playing music with your own instruments. Rec-

MODERN TRANSPORTATION

ords and radio were nearly a century away in the year 1800.

Just as important as these changes

in the way people in our culture live their everyday lives are the changes that have taken place in the way we think of the world around us. Developments in transportation and communication make the world seem ''smaller'' than it used to be; what happens thousands of miles away now has much more effect on us than it would have had 200 years ago.

We have been able to solve some of the oldest problems facing mankind with the new technology that has been developed over the past 200 years or so. Diseases that used to kill thousands, or even millions, of people in a single year are now very rare in most of the world; and people live much longer on the average today than they did two centuries ago. Man has even found ways to fly through the air much faster than any bird ever flew, and we have built machines that can take us to the moon and beyond.

With all these wonderful things, there are still many problems facing us and our cultures. New medicines and increased food production allow more humans to live longer, but so many people are living so long that our planet is becoming overcrowded. And the rockets that have carried people to the moon can also carry bombs that could someday destroy humanity and perhaps most other forms of life on Earth.

That's why it is so important that we stop sometimes to take a look at ourselves and the things we are doing. By studying ourselves we can find ways of changing cultures so that we humans don't end up as the dinosaurs of the future.